MANAGING THE ACADEMIC ENTERPRISE

MANAGING THE ACADEMIC ENTERPRISE

Case Studies for Deans and Provosts

Elwood B. Ehrle
John B. Bennett

American Council on Education • Macmillan Publishing Company
NEW YORK

Collier Macmillan Publishers
LONDON

Copyright © 1988 by American Council on Education/
Macmillan Publishing Company, A Division of Macmillan, Inc.

The American Council on Education/Macmillan Series on Higher
Education

Macmillan Publishing Company
A Division of Macmillan, Inc.
866 Third Avenue, New York, N.Y. 10022

Collier Macmillan Canada, Inc.

Library of Congress Catalog Card Number: 87-7877

Printed in the United States of America

printing number
1   2   3   4   5   6   7   8   9   10

Library of Congress Cataloging-in-Publication Data

Ehrle, Elwood B.
   Managing the academic enterprise.

   (American Council on Education/Macmillan series on
higher education)
   Includes index.
   1. Universities and colleges—United States—
Administration.   I. Bennett, John B. (John Beecher),
1940–   .   II. Title.   III. Series: American Council
on Education/Macmillan series in higher education.
LB2341.E49   1987   378.73   87-7877
ISBN 0-02-902640-7

Contents

v

Preface

In RECENT YEARS, a substantial and growing literature to guide the development of department chairpersons in American colleges and universities has been published. There has also been a steady supply of memoirs from retired college and university presidents. What has not yet appeared is a core set of practical case studies to guide the development of the middle and upper level managers of the academic enterprise—i.e., deans, chief academic or instructional officers, and provosts. This book is designed to fill that void.

Its occasional protestations to the contrary, the academy still behaves as though yesterday's good professor will ipso facto be tomorrow's good chair. In like manner, it continues to act on the theory that yesterday's good chair will be tomorrow's successful dean or provost. These beliefs persist in faculty folk wisdom even though most people who have occupied any of these positions for even a brief time recognize the limitations of this way of thinking.

A variety of journal articles have addressed various components of the dean's and provost's role, as have a large number of sessions at the annual meetings of educational associations. These are often quite helpful to individuals in these positions or those who aspire to them. Rarely, though, are these materials easily available to a wider audience, and too frequently they are limited to a very specific context.

This problem can be partially resolved through a book that directly and concretely addresses the leadership, management, and administrative concerns of deans and provosts. It is our intent to deal with these important aspects of academic life. We will do so through case studies of the kinds of situations deans and provosts encounter regularly in their work, along with responses by other deans and provosts willing to share their expertise with colleagues.

We have not produced a handbook or a compendium of research studies. The materials that follow are more personal. They can be used to stimulate self-examination and reassessment of the roles of academic officers by experienced practitioners as well as by new recruits to these important positions. Some of the issues presented are basically financial, created by insufficient resources. Others, however, turn on personnel issues, organizational structure, curricular direction, or academic freedom and standards—issues that can arise independently of financial resources. The various responses to the case studies show clearly that different leadership styles can produce very different approaches and—sometimes—very different results.

As with most authors, we are indebted to those who have come before. They are many in number and diverse in kind, too many and too diverse to cite here. To all those who have helped to shape our thought and experience, we extend our continuing thanks.

In preparing this book we acquired a new appreciation for the academic officers of our colleges and universities. We asked quite a few busy deans, provosts, and other college and university officers to take time from their overly crowded schedules to prepare responses to the twenty-five case studies around which the book is built. It was a great pleasure to see so many step forward, willing and able to take part in our project. In addition to writing fine responses, they often served as a reality check on the case studies we prepared. On several occasions, one or more called or wrote to say, "Strange that you should send me this particular case study. I have a situation in my office right now that parallels it so closely it's uncanny!"

We are also indebted to James Murray at the American Council on Education and Lloyd Chilton at the Macmillan Publishing Company for their early encouragement. Finally, we are indebted to our wives, Nancy and Elizabeth, who provided the kind of spiritual nurture and emotional support, not to mention many hours of manuscript revision, that made this book possible.

The errors, of course, are ours. In matters of interpretation and construction, we may have erred. If so, we earnestly request your indulgence. We write out of our lifelong love for the academy, and wish it and you well. It is our sincere hope that you will find these pages to be useful as you contemplate the future of the academy and your role in it.

Elwood B. Ehrle
Kalamazoo, Michigan

John B. Bennett
Adrian, Michigan

January 1987

CHAPTER ONE
Roles and Relationships

ACADEMIC OFFICERS come in many shapes and sizes. There are deans of the lower division and deans of the upper division. There are undergraduate deans and graduate deans. There are deans of research and deans of continuing education, deans of arts and sciences, and deans of the professional schools. There are misnamed deans who are really not academic officers. And there are program and area directors who really are.

The reporting relationships among academic officers are no less confusing. For instance, the chief academic officer can also be the college academic dean—as at many smaller liberal arts institutions—or the one to whom many college deans report—as at the larger comprehensive or research institutions. In the latter case, he or she is often called the vice president or vice chancellor for academic affairs, although some are known instead—or also— as provost or dean of faculties. The latter two titles can be especially bewildering, for there is no uniform practice among institutions. Sometimes the titles designate an individual on a level with other college deans, all of whom report to a chief academic officer.

It is important to recognize at the outset that many kinds of titles are applied to college and university officers, including the chief academic officer. This is because these people perform many quite different jobs. Although they may occupy the same functional level, deans and their jobs are not all alike. The arts and sciences dean in a mid-sized university may preside over a college of twen-

1

ty-five departments with 500 to 1,000 faculty members, while the
professional school or college deans in the same institution may
have four or five departments with 100 to 200 faculty members.
The difference between the "academic deans"–those who have
departments, chairpersons, and faculty reporting to or through
them–and the graduate and continuing education deans—who do
not have such built-in followings—is substantial.

Academic Deans and Provosts

Even within the group of academic deans, subtle but pervasive
differences abound. While all must deal with the trinity of budgets,
personnel, and programs, the kinds of issues faced by an engineering dean are often quite different from those faced by a fine
arts dean. The arts and sciences deanship, pervaded as it is with
the sustenance of the liberal arts tradition, is very different from
the deanship of a college of education necessarily attentive to the
elementary and secondary schools. The kinds of people attracted
to the jobs are also quite different. The temperament, values, and
operating style of the dean of a school of health, physical education,
and recreation are likely to be fundamentally different from those
of the dean of a school of business in the same institution. However, the common title "dean" often masks this fact. Recognition
of these differences is a necessary part of understanding the dynamics of academic administration, management, and leadership
in colleges and universities.

    Chief academic officers are also a diverse group. For the pur-
poses of this book, deans will be considered to head major academic or functional sectors of the institution. Unlike deans, however, there can be only one chief academic officer or provost in
an institution. The chief academic officer or provost must embrace
the concerns of the deans of all of the schools and colleges of the
institution. His or her mandate includes the management of the
entire academic enterprise. This makes for a fundamental difference between deans and chief academic officers, whether the latter
are called provosts or academic vice presidents. We will use the
title provost to refer to the chief academic officer, thereby dis-
tinguishing him or her from the academic deans to whom the

faculty report and on whose shoulders immediate responsibility for the academic programs rests.

Deans are expected to be unrelenting champions for their particular portion of the academic spectrum. Chief academic officers are expected to balance the concerns of all for the good of the whole institution. Deans have multitudes of faculty they can rally to any particular cause. Chief academic officers have primarily a handful of deans. Deans live closer to the day-to-day operations of the academic programs. Chief academic officers live closer to the president, trustees, legislators, and external constituencies. Deans work with the faculty. Chief academic officers are often isolated in what is called the "central administration."

This picture is complicated by the fact that many chief academic officers come to their positions after a successful tenure as a school or college dean. This means that the chief academic officer was socialized into the norms of business deans, arts and sciences deans, graduate deans, or some other group, and has the inherent and acquired biases of that group. Some chief academic officers rise above these biases more easily than others. Some overcompensate and thereby cause anxiety in the very group from which they have come. If one has been an arts and sciences dean for a number of years, and resisted the expansion of the professional schools at the expense of the liberal arts, it may be difficult to take an entirely new posture on this issue when the job title changes to chief academic officer.

In many institutions the chief academic officer is recognized as the number two person behind the president in scope and authority. If his or her primary title is vice president for academic affairs, the number two role is not always warmly accepted by other vice presidents—for example, those of finance, student affairs, and government relations. Where the number two role is accepted, the common title is provost. It is not at all unusual to see an individual bearing the title vice president for academic affairs *and* provost.

Personal Requirements

Whatever the title, the dean or provost fulfills a wide variety of responsibilities. Basically, the academic officer is expected to function as the academic conscience for his or her unit of administration, the dean for his or her college, and the provost for the university. Within the organization it is he or she to whom others look for assurance that the right things are being done and done correctly. The individual academic officer usually subscribes to this view as well. The combination of responsibilities and expectations can require one to draw upon a wide variety of professional and personal competencies.

Management abilities and academic insight are two crucial and quite different requirements. Most academic institutions have become very complex organizations, often with large bureaucracies. In this context, achieving and maintaining academic integrity requires considerable management versatility and skills in planning, budgetary affairs, and conflict resolution, as well as interpersonal sensitivities and judgment, not to mention a good measure of luck. We will look at some very specific illustrations of these management characteristics as we examine the case studies in the following chapters.

Sophisticated managerial skills alone are insufficient. Academic insight and vision are just as important. Faculty frequently persist in speaking and thinking of the institution as though it were still some idyllic college in which reason and goodness reign. From this perspective, the only administrative requirement is additional resources, which should be quickly and fairly distributed to those departments and areas, usually their own, that obviously have greater needs! For academic leaders to get things done, this mythology must be honored at the same time it is circumvented. Walking this tightrope is not easy. It requires incorporating the mythology into a larger vision.

Another challenge involves the levers of collegial control—levers that are never very evident or easily worked. Faculty members vary greatly in industry, cooperativeness, and commitment to teamwork. Some possess dispositions that can only be called cranky. Many seem suspicious of anything new or different, particularly if it is associated with the provost or dean. The faculty senate committee structure often reinforces these difficulties. Securing faculty support for an idea or project can take time and energy completely out of proportion to the value of the outcome.

Accordingly, academic officers must have a healthy self-confidence. Faculty are not inclined to provide great support. As one author notes, "Although football teams recognize their need for quarterbacks, academic faculties perpetuate the fantasy that they succeed more or less on their own. A dean must be able to live gracefully with that untruth."[1] For most deans and chief academic officers, the ability to maintain a low profile will be required. Only a few of the truly flamboyant will survive. The rest must be prepared to give credit to faculty, even for their own ideas.

Key Constituencies: The Professoriate

The primary constituency for the academic officer is the faculty. Depending on the issue, it can also be the decisive constituency. The dean or vice president is not hired by the faculty, but he or she is rarely hired without them and certainly cannot last long when positioned too often against them.

The challenges facing the professoriate—and therefore the academic officer—are enormous.[2] At the top of the list is a perceived loss of public status, together with an eroding self-esteem and sense of security. A relative decline of income reinforces the sense of slipping public respect. The purchasing power of today's salary has shrunk compared with that of ten and fifteen years ago. Many faculty members find their purchasing power eroding just as their own children come to their collegiate years.

These matters are complicated by the loss of excitement that a considerable number of faculty feel as the reality of their immobility becomes apparent. For many, their first full-time academic job will be their only academic job. What may have been taken as a temporary position immediately after graduate school fifteen or twenty years ago has developed into an endlessly permanent position. The loss of excitement is compounded by a sense of reduced student preparation—and perhaps capacity—and by the apparent reduction in the number of students genuinely interested in study for its own sake. An increasing number of faculty members are experiencing the numbing consequences of various combinations of these factors.

These are important factors, especially when taken together. At a number of institutions, the shift of values regarding research and scholarly opportunities and expectations creates further anxiety for faculty. Many affiliated with institutions noted for teaching excellence are now finding a variety of pressures to do more research and publication. Peter Seldin's research suggests that increasing attention is being paid to such accomplishments at undergraduate institutions.[3] Yet faculty are often ill-prepared to undertake research after years away from graduate school. And others, though able and interested, are not provided the freedom, the funds, or the tools.

At the same time, those in research institutions are increasingly finding that funding and support for research projects are less available. The number of proposals approved but not funded is growing. Those of middle years at such institutions may find themselves experiencing lessening degrees of satisfaction in what had earlier been rewarding and fulfilling roles. Some research institutions are displaying renewed attention to the importance of teaching effectiveness, without providing sufficient assistance to those working under an earlier set of rewards and rules.

In both types of institutions, finding ways to maintain faculty motivation and promote risk-taking and growth becomes imperative for academic officers. Deans and provosts must work together to advance these goals. At the same time, strains between older and younger faculty continue, as do differentiations between disciplines that are a function of market forces. Collegiality is under increasing stress and is likely to be reduced. The continued extension of collective bargaining has exacerbated these challenges at some institutions. Morris's general observation about faculty is still probably quite true: "As a group, faculty members do not consider themselves hard to get along with. They are not inclined to entertain the possibility that they are strong-willed, now and then unreasonable, sometimes irascible and unpleasant, and on some occasions downright dishonest."[4]

In the midst of all this, the academic officer needs to oversee faculty evaluation and development and ensure that they are indeed melded. Issues of post-tenure evaluation, contract differcntiation, and quality control for adjunct and part-time faculty are becoming more important. Although escalating developments in technology could, in theory, easily alter much of the traditional instructional practice and environment, the chances are greater that change will occur gradually rather than abruptly.

The traditional faculty focus on process—including committee work, reflection, discussion, and achieving consensus—means that change is difficult. Time is not viewed as money; the new is often branded as only a fad and something to resist. As a result of their high level of dependence on multiple faculty constituencies, academic officers often feel quite vulnerable. Developments for which they may feel—and in fact are charged with—responsibility, but over which they actually have no direct control, can contribute to periodic malaise and impatience.

In spite of all these difficulties, a soft-spoken, understated, and self-effacing nobility of purpose illuminates the professoriate. While it is true that many faculty members are troubled and troublesome, it is also true that many are enthusiastic, excited about learning, capable, committed, and ready and cheerfully able to get on with the work of educating the next generation. They exist in considerable numbers and provide the energy whereby higher education dares to continue with its difficult task. Because the dean and provost, by the very nature of their positions, serve as lightning rods drawing out the anger, frustration, and conflict in their faculty colleagues, it is imperative that they remind themselves frequently of the values and high purpose that drew them into the academic profession in the first place and caused them to opt for a leadership role within it. It is especially important that deans and provosts see beyond the issues of the day to the high ideals that cause a faculty member to become cantankerous. Beneath the surface of every troubled professor lies a rock-hard commitment to the importance of the work he or she does. Were this not so, deans and provosts could not long endure, nor could the academic enterprise they seek to lead.

Despite the challenges and frustrations, the typical academic officer feels a primordial and inalienable bond with the faculty. He or she comes from the faculty and often envisions some day returning to it.

Key Constituencies: The Department Chairpersons

A key constituency for any college dean is the department or division chairpersons. The provost or academic vice president is more removed from those in these positions. It is a key constituency for the dean because it is precisely the point where institutional services are actually delivered. Institutions succeed or fail because of what happens in departments.

At too many institutions, chairpersons come to the position without preparation, work in relative isolation from each other—each one burdened by the assumption that he or she is laboring in singular circumstances—and often serve with inadequate institutional attention or reward for accomplishments. Ironically, expectations for chairs have increased at many of these same institutions, as responsibilities for staffing night classes and weekend colleges have been added to oversight of regular daytime courses and activities.

The relative lack of visible institutional concern about chairpersons, as well as the paucity of support provided them, is surprising in our educational institutions. Fortunately, there is mounting evidence in the last few years that things have started to change. A major national program of two-day workshops for both new and experienced chairpersons was launched by the American Council on Education in 1980. Offered both regionally and on individual campuses, these workshops provide appropriate management skills and the more basic recognition of the importance of those who serve. The Center for Faculty Development and Evaluation at Kansas State University now offers an annual conference for department and division chairs. Several book-length publications dealing with issues faced by chairs, as well as two national newsletters, have appeared in the last few years.[5]

Still, problems remain. For instance, a large percentage of those surveyed report serving as chairs to the detriment of their own career advancement. Likewise, selection of department chairs remains difficult at many institutions. Too often, those who have an expressed interest in serving are regarded by colleagues as too ambitious. Those with little interest are then pressed into service, and subsequently show an understandable lack of enthusiasm or attention to the job.

College deans need to be sensitive to the role-ambiguity that department chairs periodically feel. Independent of whether they were selected by appointment or election, chairs have most of the same responsibilities for curricular adequacy; for faculty recruitment, evaluation, and development; and for appropriate department direction and standards. The work of the academic dean will be immeasurably facilitated by the success of chairs in these areas. Deans need to remember that in meeting these responsibilties, chairs almost inevitably feel divided loyalties to faculty colleagues and to institutional administrators.

Chairs also need to realize that the role-ambiguity inherent in their positions may be among their greatest blessings. A variety of experiences suggest that when attempts are made to "clarify" the dimensions of this ambiguity, chairs are more boxed in than they usually want to be. Part of the magic in the chairs' position lies in their ability to "work both sides of the street." The resulting conceptual and operational latitude should not be easily given away. Although chairs will periodcially believe that role-ambiguity is hampering their effectiveness, deans can help them to see that this isn't the case at all. With effective communication, the apparent role-ambiguity experienced by chairs can be used to the continuing benefit of both deans and chairs. Where communication isn't effective, it should be recognized as a problem to be dealt with rather than hiding it under the cover of role-ambiguity.

Deans who report to provosts or to vice presidents for academic affairs are in several respects like department chairpersons who report to deans. The chairs in their colleges are the deans' major constituency, as the department faculty are the major constituency of the chairs. Chairs, like faculty, can be quite cool toward a hierarchical command structure. Deans, therefore, are in a good position to know the leadership challenges facing their own chairpersons.

For his or her part, the chief academic officer needs to observe some of the same things that the college dean must with faculty— for instance, not permitting, and certainly not encouraging, individuals to bypass the dean. Bypassing is profoundly discouraging to the dean and a radically inefficient use of the dean's position.

One of the overriding challenges for both deans and chairs is loyalty. Faculty, especially at the larger institutions, know that their scholarly reputations are usually established outside the institution, and so may be disposed to view the department or college mainly as a platform for this larger audience. Their energies become devoted primarily to the discipline and secondarily to the campus. Just as the chairs have both an opportunity and need to create a distinctive entity out of an aggregate of individuals with competing and sometimes conflicting interests, so must the dean forge one entity out of the various departments. The college dean has the opportunity to create a shared spirit among the chairs. By doing so, the dean puts his or her personal stamp on the organization through the values promoted and worked for. In responding to this opportunity, chairs are a natural and indispensable ally. The wise academic dean will recognize this and enlist them.

The college dean can find himself or herself confronted with the same tensions that chairs face between advocacy for the collegial unit and loyalty to the larger institutional context. The tension can be poignant when institutional budgetary constraints or changing missions force the dean to balance the requirements of his or her college or school with the broader institutional perspective, thereby participating in the diminution of the former.

Another respect in which chairs and college deans share organizational similarities is the competition among their respective peers for institutional resources. Chairs ultimately vie with each other for limited school or college monies for special projects and equipment as well as for ongoing general support. College deans are in a similar situation and fight some of the same battles. The dean of humanities or of arts and sciences, for instance, knows the difficulties in contesting for resources and influence with the deans of the professional schools. Organizational charts are misleading in that their equally sized boxes suggest equal influence and importance.

In this connection, much of the same advice given elsewhere to chairs applies also to college deans.[6] The reputation one establishes for reliability and consistency counts significantly in coloring the provost's disposition to grant or withhold requests. The college dean must tread the same narrow line as the chair between providing insufficient information and providing so much supporting detail that the cutting edge of the request is blunted. Of course, both chairpersons and chief academic officers need cultivating and stroking. Deans, like chairs, must "work both sides of the street."

The specific constituencies of a school dean can be a function of historical accident, earlier budgetary pressures, or personality conflicts. At one midwestern institution, there is a dean of the school of nursing and mathematics! One can only guess at the circumstances and dimensions of an earlier institutional trauma that produced such a combination.

Special situations will also arise, sometimes with unexpected frequency. Chairs may have to cope with former chairs still in the department and unhappy at their loss of power. Occasionally, there will be a former dean in the department, sometimes one who has stepped down unwillingly. Academic deans need to be sensitive to these developments and willing to suggest and support appropriate initiatives.

Deans need to pay attention to the development needs of chairpersons as much as to those of faculty. Periodic workshops on faculty and staff development, fund raising, affirmative action techniques, or time-and-stress management can be valuable activities, especially if they are identified as desirable by chairs in earlier surveys. Deans should also be attentive to the personal needs of chairs, sensitive to their individual situations, and prepared to provide as much support as possible to permit ongoing scholarly vigor and continued teaching effectiveness.

As Warren notes, deans need to pay attention to communicating the "philosophical moorings" of their relationship with chairs along with being alert to the teaching roles of leaders generally. Too much communication is conducted at the level of the mechanical and the routine. Likewise, "the dean must take the lead in reducing the amount of unproductive record keeping expected of the chairperson."[7] In these various ways the dean can maximize beneficial working relationships with his or her chairpersons—a constituency, like the faculty, that one simply cannot for long afford to alienate.

Key Constituencies: The President

Unlike department chairs, except at single-college institutions, deans report to a chief academic officer. This reporting relationship often involves far more of a hierarchical character than that between chairs and deans. The deans of the professional schools, the college of arts and sciences, the graduate school, and continuing education must deal with an individual who quite likely functions under a different organizational logic.

The chief academic officer has the chief institutional officer as his or her major constituency. Success or failure in that relationship may much more immediately affect job satisfaction and tenure than do relationships with the other constituenices. Certainly, the academic officer must look to the president to receive authority commensurate with responsibility as well as support for the authority exercised.

As Wolverton observes, presidents and chief academic officers need to be "in philosophical and pragmatic agreement at least 80 to 85 percent of the time."[8] More than this risks a "yes-man" relationship, while less can result in excessive stress. Presidents depend upon chief academic officers to keep them sufficiently informed to maintain credibility both on and off campus. There must be mutual trust, respect, and reliance.

It is perhaps unfortunate that academic vice presidents and provosts usually do not have the opportunity to work with several different presidents in several different institutions. If they did, they would have a greater opportunity to know how incredibly diverse presidents are. A broader view of the spectrum of presidential types would go a long way in helping them to gauge the strengths and weaknesses of their particular president.

Believe it or not, presidents, too , may feel stuck in their roles. They may have worked most of their lives to get where they are only to discover that the presidential role, as they have come to perceive it, doesn't fit very well. Some presidents are sorely troubled by the experienced loss of academic freedom as they have climbed upward in the system. It is fairly clear that the amount of academic freedom an individual has is inversely related to his or her height in the system. An assistant professor can advocate free love, divestiture of South African stocks, abortion on demand, the cessation of all nuclear research, or any number of other things. Chairs and deans have less freedom to say what they think. Presidents have almost none.

Fortunately for American higher education, the great majority of college and university presidents are capable, committed, and seasoned people who are ready, willing, and able to lead their institutions. There are exceptions, of course. There are dictatorial types among presidents who provide, in their minds if not in their statements, Charles de Gaulle's famous rationale for any of their positions or actions. For them, "Je suis le President!" says it all. There are anxious and fearful types who are so afraid of controversy that they fill little more than the figure-head component of the role. There are preretirement types who have long since retired mentally and allowed their institution to drift aimlessly. Finally, there are consummate politicians for whom winning at intrigue is more important than the issues involved. Since the president-provost relationship is so important to the health of the institution, every provost should periodically reassess which categories fit the president with whom he or she works. Presidents do change their basic views and style, although not very often. External consultants can be useful in helping provosts to maintain a productive posture vis-à-vis that of their president.

Key Constituencies: Boards, Systems, and Legislators

The nature of boards of trustees deserves more careful attention than has been provided heretofore. Much of the available literature is generated by trustees or by associations of governing boards. While most of this is of considerable value, some of the changes occurring in boards can be adequately gauged only through sustained study by external observers.

Perhaps the most important aspect of college and university boards is their intensely political nature. Whether appointed by governors, elected by the people of a state, or derived from wealthy or influential benefactors in a "self-perpetuating board" mode, boards and their individual members have various histories, intents, and public and hidden agendas. There are likely to be in-groups and out-groups on most college and university boards. In some extreme cases there may be a "local mafia" controlling the board and considerable resentment from nonlocal trustees.

A second critically important aspect of a board is its level of understanding of the difference between policy and management. While policy is a board prerogative, involvement in day-to-day management is not, or at least *should* not be. Each board member is likely to have a somewhat different view on this subject. Some board members hold to the view that the only involvement trustees should have in management is the selection, support, and eventual replacement of the president. Others believe it is their mandate to examine any administrative action that comes to their attention.

A third important aspect of a board is its need to present a unified public face. Not infrequently, beneath its public solidarity are a number of bitter and protracted conflicts. Woe to the provost who doesn't know that the ouster of his or her president is being hotly but privately debated by a board, with the president's continuance hanging by a very slim thread.

A fourth aspect of boards lies in their scope of control. They may be responsible for a single institution, a small group of somewhat homogeneous institutions or, as is the case in a number of states, all of the public institutions in the state. In the former case, board members are more likely to be informed in detail about the activities of the institutions. In the latter case, their involvement is more likely to be from a distance, and their knowledge of the details of the operation of each institution in their charge considerably more limited.

Where a number of institutions is involved, the state board deals with the individual institutions through an agency frequently referred to as the "state system office." These agencies are clearly a mixed blessing.

In states with one giant prestigious institution and several to many less-complex colleges and universities, there is probably merit in the smaller institutions' approaching the legislature on fiscal matters through a state system office. In states with two or more educational giants, contention with one another may result in a better deal for everyone without much influence from a state board or state system office.

When legislatures allocate funds for the institutions to a state board or a state system office, the Golden Rule applies. "He who has the gold makes the rules!" This is likely to create an even larger state system bureaucracy, which may lead to yet more rules. These matters are further complicated in a state where collective bargaining practice is "coordinated." When a statewide bargaining unit is negotiating with the state personnel office, both the individual campuses and the state higher education system office may be reduced to onlookers.

It may still be too soon to determine whether the move toward state boards, state system offices, and statewide bargaining units is a good thing or not. Periodically, legislation is introduced in one state or another to abolish such entities. The bills usually die in committee. It appears likely that these agencies will be around for some time. Mixed blessing or not, deans and provosts need to understand them and learn how to work creatively with them.

Finally, deans and provosts should always remember that board members get their information from a wide variety of sources—official and unofficial. It does little good to try gently to persuade students or faculty to avoid end-running the entire academic structure by carrying their concerns to a board member. When they are concerned enough, they will go to a board member, and the president or provost is likely to receive a call from a board member of the "I understand that such and such is taking place and I want to know what you intend to do about it" type. Each such occasion invites trustees further into the details of day-to-day management than is good for the institution. It does little good to tell a board member that you wish he or she hadn't been called. The only recourse the provost has is temporarily to abandon other priorities and deal with the board member's concern. In so doing, the provost must do his or her homework to a fare-thee-well, even while regretting that it has become necessary to take time out to do it at all.

The same sort of difficulty is attached to unpredictable calls from members of the state legislative bodies. When a call comes in indicating that "This is Senator A, B, or C's office and we would like to know about x, y, or z," the provost usually has to get moving, even when the call comes into the president's office.

Like trustees, some legislators have superb academic credentials and a long history of experience with academic institutions. Also like trustees, some do not. In either case, while the president and vice president for government relations are gently coaching legislators and trustees alike in the difference between policy and day-to-day operations, the provost often has to "get busy" and answer their detailed inquiries anyway.

In spite of the occasional messiness of these matters, there is likely to be a strong and genuinely ingenious reason for their recurrence. It may well be that " . . . the academy is just too important to be left entirely to the academics." We should all be thankful that this, indeed, seems to be the case.

Organization Of the Case Study Chapters

Each of the case study chapters (2–6) presents five case studies. Each case study is preceded by a brief introduction and followed by responses from two or three current or recently retired deans or provosts and brief comments by the authors. The nature, origin, and possible uses of the case studies is described at the beginning of Chapter 2.

Although the case studies were organized into chapters with general themes in mind, their sequence is somewhat arbitrary. Other organizations and sequences suggested themselves but were rejected in favor of retaining this somewhat arbitrary arrangement to better reflect what actually happens in deans' and provosts' offices. The issues that crowd the academic officer's calendar do not appear in neat sequences allowing the luxury of treating related things together. A degree of randomness is present in every working day. Thus, while we are happy to acknowledge that other chapter organizations are possible or perhaps even desirable, we are comfortable with the notion that the reader will probably skip around in the chapters anyway.

As you move through the case study chapters, you will notice that there is considerable diversity in the nature of the responses offered by current or recently retired deans and provosts. Some are highly structured and methodically laid out. Others are conversational and casual. Some may say too much; others not quite enough. We did not edit the responses for either structural or stylistic uniformity. Rather, we have elected to celebrate the diversity of types of people filling deans' and provosts' roles by letting each speak in his or her own way. There is a marvelous richness in this diversity. Thus, the differences in the responses reflect the real world in a rather direct way. We applaud and celebrate the underlying diversity and invite you to measure yourself against it as you peruse the case study chapters.

Notes

1. Van Cleve Morris, *Deaning: Middle Management in Academe* (Urbana: University of Illinois Press, 1981), p. 24.
2. Jack H. Schuster and Howard R. Bowen, "The Faculty at Risk," *Change* (Sept/Oct, 1985), pp. 13–21.
3. Peter Seldin, *Changing Practices in Faculty Evaluation* (San Francisco: Jossey-Bass, 1984), pp. 33–74.
4. Morris, p. 18.
5. Three books have recently appeared: David B. Booth, *The Department Chair: Professional Development and Role Conflict*, AAHE-ERIC Higher Education Research Report 10, 1982; John B. Bennett, *Managing the Academic Department: Cases and Notes* (New York: ACE/Macmillan, 1983); and Allan Tucker, *Chairing the Academic Department*, 2nd ed. (New York: ACE/Macmillan, 1984). Two newsletters with national circulation are *The Department Advisor*, available from P.O. Box 12635, Denver, Colorado 80212, and *The Academic Leader*, available from 607 North Sherman Avenue, Madison, Wisconsin 53704.
6. See Charles O. Warren, "Chairperson and Dean: The Essential Partnership," *The Department Advisor* (Winter, 1986), pp. 6–8, and John B. Bennett, "A Chairperson's Notes to the Dean," *AAHE Bulletin* (June, 1982), pp. 15–16.
7. Warren, p. 7.
8. Robert E. Wolverton, "The Chief Academic Officer: Argus on the Campus," in *Leadership Roles of Chief Academic Officers*, ed. David G. Brown (San Francisco: Jossey-Bass, 1984), p. 8.

CHAPTER TWO

The Academic Players: Provost, Dean, Department Chairs, and Faculty

AS INDICATED in the first chapter, operational effectiveness in many academic leadership positions usually depends on the nature of the relationships among and between the occupants of these positions. Chapters 2 through 6 explore the nature of these relationships via case studies accompanied by responses prepared by knowledgeable and experienced practitioners.

One of the respondents made the following observation. "All the good advice in the world does not add up to as useful a tool as a sensitive appreciation for the subtle nuances of personality and power which operate within the structures of our institutions." This is quite true. One's intuitions are shaped by concrete experience in the situation and with the players. One's sense of likely outcomes is sharpened by reflection on what has happened before and by deepening appreciation of subtle dimensions of the personalities of others. Precisely because they lack such detailed, even intimate, concrete particularity, case studies can instruct by forcing us to go beyond the vague assurances that *this* person will

19

act in *that* way. We are invited, rather, to take inventory of the
the range of responses a variety of persons would likely display.

As the same respondent also observes, "I have credits and
debits I have accumulated with faculty, other administrators, student groups, trustees, etc., which will help to define the scope
or the limits of what I can do, and the same holds true for each
of us." On the other hand, looking at the cases described, without
the need or the ability to cash in one's chits, relieves the reader
of some of the burdens administrators must otherwise carry.

The case studies were developed from various experiences of
the authors or their associates over the years. In several cases,
different experiences were melded to create the dynamics of the
case study. While none of the case studies presents the full detail
of an actual occurrence in an identifiable institution, all of them
are based in one way or another on real experiences. In several
instances, respondents to the case studies wrote or called one of
the authors to indicate that they had been involved recently in a
situation similar to the one for which we had asked them to prepare
a response.

The case studies can be used in a variety of ways. Some will
find them interesting and at times amusing personal reading.
Others will want to use them to encourage discussion of particular
situations. In preparing their responses, several respondents indicated that they "assigned" a case study to colleagues and then
discussed the thinking behind their colleagues' various responses.
The case studies can also be used in various combinations in leadership development workshops and other types of administrative
development programs. Faculty may find them useful in obtaining
a fuller view of the kinds of situations their administrators deal
with on a day-to-day basis.

The case studies in this chapter begin to deal with the relationships between and among the several academic players who
might be involved in any given situation. As in a kaleidoscope,
particular alignments among them seem always to be shifting
somewhat, reflecting now this and now that combination. Sometimes, the causal agents of these shifts in alignment are financial
or territorial in character. Sometimes, though, they reflect personality differences, disagreements in basic academic value judg-

ments, or disparate management philosophies or perspectives. In any case, deans or provosts are likely, on occasion, to find themselves situated over against members of a subgroup who attach more importance to their group traditions and prospects than to those of the larger collegial context. It is important in dealing with each new situation to pause and ask who the various players are and what their interests are likely to be.

Strengthening Departmental Responsibility

The first case study describes a situation involving uncritical department promotion recommendations. Several factors are at issue. The question of the dual responsibilities of the chair is especially evident, as is the need for the dean to identify more effective communication strategies.

CASE STUDY

It was the third time in as many years that Arts and Sciences Dean Bob Shuman had received uncritical promotion recommendations from the psychology department. As before, the chair had simply passed along the department vote and had attached no really independent analysis of his own. It was all too clear that the faculty of the psychology department had uncommonly high regard for each other—a regard that Shuman did not share. As a whole, he judged the department to be merely adequate. There were certainly other departments within the college that Shuman considered to be of superior quality, ones that enjoyed good reputations for strong curricular offerings and for displaying some scholarly excitement. Neither feature was especially characteristic of the psychology faculty.

Shuman had discussed the departmental profile with its chair on earlier occasions and had been told that the time and energy required for the general education distribution and service courses had worked against developing a larger departmental reputation. Shuman had not been converted to this view then, nor had he changed his mind since. It was true that the department was dependable and the faculty reasonably conscientious toward students and committee responsibilities. There was no excitement, however, associated with the department. Facing declining enrollments and faculty stagflation, the college needed all the excitement it could generate.

Preoccupied by other matters, Shuman had let the issue ride. Now, though, the failure of the department chair to bite the bullet on a promotion recommendation to full professor reminded Shuman of the need to do something. At the very least, the chair needed to take more responsibility on promotion matters. After all, the chair had a responsibility to the institution as much as he did to his faculty colleagues. The associate professor candidate was a nice enough person, but his qualifications for promotion to full professor were barely beyond the minimum, and certainly far from exemplary.

Neither of the previous department recommendations had received favorable institutional action. Now it appeared that the chair had not gotten the message or had chosen to ignore it.

The faculty handbook criteria were not much help. They were precise enough on establishing time-in-rank for eligibility, but quite general in setting forth performance criteria to guide judgments once eligibility was established. Even so, the other departments and chairs were holding to standards that Dean Shuman found to be quite acceptable. Why, Shuman wondered, should he make an exception for psychology?

It seemed that another talk about the department profile wouldn't help. How should the dean proceed?

Response # 1

It is easy to sympathize with Dean Shuman. He faces the difficult tasks of transforming a department that is not aware of its need to be transformed and of dealing effectively with a department chair who was happy to assume the rights of the position, but not ready to assume in equal fashion the responsibilities that go with it. Now Bob Shuman must have a long talk with the chair of the psychology department, where the essential message will be a negative one. But he also knows that the department chair must leave that meeting with something positive and with a recognition that there are good things that can come out of his acceptance of the responsibilities that go with his position.

Dean Shuman should not support the department's (and the department chair's) recommendation concerning this promotion. Two earlier recommendations had not received favorable action, and this one should not either. In fact, Dean Shuman can use this third turn-down to good advantage. It is bound to have a negative, if not devastating, impact on departmental morale. But a plus can come out of this situation if the department chair can be encouraged to provide leadership in the department so that he can take some of the credit for overcoming these problems.

Prior to Dean Shuman's meeting with the department chair, he first needs to do his homework. He should have available to share with the chair a history of recent promotion activities within the college and university, and he should use this factual information as a way to discuss both the individual criteria and the larger departmental ingredients in positive promotion situations. This should be done in a way that plays down the sense that he is taking the department chair to task. It should be designed to bring him into an active conversation with the dean about what is needed for positive promotion action and why.

Second, the dean should come prepared to speak affirmatively about contributions the psychology department and its program make to the college. This should include contributions not only of the more traditional kind within the major, but also the general education function that psychology plays in the programs of the institution. The department chair should not be given the impression that the dean thinks the department is making no contribution, but he should get the clear message that the value of those contributions and their recognition by the university can be enhanced through stronger departmental activity.

In the context of these two preliminary strategies, the dean will be in a position to call on the department chair again to lead the department back into the mainstream of the university's academic life. The dean should do this, not simply by pointing out his specific expectations (although it is important to do this), but also by finding ways to support faculty within the department who are interested in renewal. He should be ready to commit discretionary monies that may be in his budget, if only in modest amounts, to members of the psychology department who show themselves interested in enhanced roles within the discipline and within the institution. He may also wish to ask the department chair to involve the entire department in a program review to

spot strengths and weaknesses in what the department does. Finally, he should approach the department chair and encourage
him to function as a partner with the dean in assisting the faculty
of the department to become stronger and more creative con-
tributors to the institution's curriculum. If the department chair
can be brought to see the positive benefits to him and to his
colleagues of this new leadership role, he will be in a better position to see the debilitating impact on his department that has
arisen from simply affirming the status quo. Such a delicate mix-
ture of displeasure and support should be the formative principle
of Dean Shuman's planning for his meeting with the department
chair. (G. Benjamin Oliver, Dean of Arts and Sciences, Southwestern University, Georgetown, Texas.)

Response # 2

This case study illustrates an all-too-familiar problem. Every academic officer has faced it, but the options depend very much
on a number of details that are not given in the brief case study.

First, the dean needs to consider what makes the department
so unexciting. If this is a research institution, is the major problem
that this faculty is low on research output by comparison with
other departments in the college? If it is not a research institution,
what does the department lack compared with other departments
that met with greater favor in Dean Shuman's eyes? The initial
step should be to assess just what the dean expects of faculty in
the departments in his college. When the dean has identified
what is lacking, he is in a position to determine possible alternative
actions.

One gets the impression that the department is made up of
faculty who have been around together for quite some time and
lost interest in their own or one another's ideas. The case study
mentions "stagflation," but does not specify how this department
is affected. The dean has reviewed the departmental profile, so
he knows whether all or most of the faculty are tenured. If there
are untenured faculty, there may be opportunities for change.
Although it may take some time to make major changes in the
department this way, the dean can certainly take advantage of
the opportunities to encourage untenured faculty to be productive, and to replace faculty who do not achieve tenure with more
promising candidates. If any faculty are likely to retire in the near

future, the dean has not only the opportunity to change the profile a bit, but also might get the chair's attention by reminding him that replacement will depend on improved productivity, increased enrollments, or whatever he is looking for.

If the faculty is fully tenured, the dean should consider making use of the college's faculty development program, or creating one if there is none. Of course, deans have discovered that the faculty who most need development or retraining are not necessarily the most eager to obtain it, so some persuasion or incentive is called for. If the institution has a tenured faculty evaluation system, the dean might be able to use it to good advantage. If the institution has a merit salary system, the dean should investigate the allocations received by the faculty of the department in question. If the faculty had received more merit pay than the dean believes their performance would suggest, he may be in a position to alter that pattern. If they had received lower-than-average merit allocations but the chair and faculty had failed to notice it (unlikely), he could call it to their attention.

It appears that the dean met with the chair on at least one occasion. A meeting with the department faculty might bring out some interesting issues. The dean should ascertain whether the department faculty had asked the previous dean for anything that he refused them, except for the promotion. Were they so satisfied that they never requested more space, a larger budget, or additional personnel? Even faculty who are well-satisfied with themselves tend to be dissatisfied with the way they are treated by the administration. Getting some of these items on the table would help to gain the faculty's attention to the dean's evaluation.

The role played by the department chair should be assessed. Has the department had the same chair for a long time? If the chair is a large part of the problem, the dean needs to know what role he can play in making a change. (Norma S. Rees, Vice Chancellor for Academic Affairs, University of Wisconsin-Milwaukee.)

The first response (Dean Oliver) draws our attention to the importance of the dean's providing affirming leadership at the same time that expectations of department improvement are effectively delivered. Emphasis is placed upon establishing a comparative context for members of the department as well as upon identifying ways to enlist the chair in attending to the broader context. The second response (Vice Chancellor Rees) extends this analysis and broadens the horizons. Both responses indicate that the dean has some homework to do before taking any action at all. It is insufficient to say that a department "lacks excitement." Unless the dean can clarify in his own mind exactly what that means for the department in question, he is severely handicapped in rectifying the situation.

Some of the tools that the dean may have available or may attempt to create include judicious use of salary and equipment awards. These should be accompanied by information about similar awards made elsewhere and the circumstances supporting them. Individuals tend to rise to the expectations of significant others, and faculty are no exception. As they better understand what is expected of them, they will strive to deliver it. This can go far in strengthening a department's view of itself.

Replacing the Dean

Departments are not the only units with leadership needs. Occasionally it is the dean or director of a school or college who needs attention. The second case study presents a situation in which decanal responsibilities may have been neglected.

CASE STUDY

Provost Straight knew that she had a problem the very first time she met the engineering dean. The man had lost his vitality some time ago. His handshake was as limp as his eyes, his posture, and his spirit. In retrospect, she had wondered about the interview grilling the trustees had given her on how she would handle engineering. At the time, she saw it as sexist on their part. Now, having come to know the dean, she was inclined to think the trustees knew all along that there was a problem in engineering but were perhaps not yet ready to admit what it was.

Dean Prior had, after all, built the engineering college from the ground up. He had been an associate professor during the period of deciding whether to convert the industrial arts teaching certificate program into technology, make a run for engineering, or phase out the whole thing. That was when Prior's leadership first became manifest, about twenty years ago. Other faculty found many reasons to accept his view that engineering was the way to go. In due course he became a full professor, then founding chair of the first engineering department, and finally dean of the college of engineering, all with a master's degree in industrial arts and two brief "how to do it" papers published years ago.

He was reasonably well-liked in the engineering college, particularly by an entrenched "don't rock the boat" senior faculty. He had many influential friends in the Rotary Club and the Chamber of Commerce, where he was one of the university's representatives, and at the golf course. Now, however, there was reason to wonder whether he had what it takes to continue to lead the college he had helped to build.

The college of engineering was up for initial accreditation—again. The earlier review had cited several weaknesses, prompting Provost Straight's predecessor to redirect a considerable amount of funding toward engineering to meet some of its shortcomings. Dean Prior lobbied well for more equipment, new laboratories, and more faculty positions, and got them, somewhat to the consternation of the other deans and an increasing number of faculty, particularly in the humanities. Some of the problem seemed to be in a seriously outmoded curriculum. Faculty committees in the college were loathe to recommend changes and, regretfully, the dean wasn't up to helping them to develop the kind of curriculum the accreditors were looking for. Young faculty learned early that if they ever wanted to make tenure, they had better not take the senior faculty to task on curricular matters. Provost Straight knew from other experiences that accrediting teams will often present long lists of shortcomings in their formal reports and only tell you privately and off the record that the real problem is the dean. That, in any case, occurred before Straight's time and was lost with her predecessor.

She felt bad about what was becoming apparent. She wasn't yet ready to formulate a plan for dealing with the engineering "situation," and knew that it wouldn't be long before the trustees asked her for one. Her tentative conversations with the president hadn't helped clarify her thinking.

It would be nice if Prior would reverse his long-held negative

view of early retirement. If he did, Straight knew that she could
sweeten the pot for him both financially and honorably. But, not
a chance. He continued to lecture anyone who would listen about
the great loss to the university when any of its senior people
retired early. His senior faculty totally supported this premise,
of course, but Straight was pretty sure he wasn't just playing to
the gallery. Prior really believed that leaving early bordered on
treason.

There hadn't been a formal evaluation of deans for as long as
anyone could remember. Straight marveled at this as she added
it to her growing list of "must do" future projects. It would have
to be approached cautiously, but it would have to be approached
nonetheless. At least she had been through one while she was
an arts and sciences dean, so she wouldn't be starting from scratch
in thinking about the process. The politics were something else.

Since Straight wasn't making much headway in clarifying her
options, she decided to call her old mentor, now several states
away. He had been provost when she became department chair
and was quite instrumental in helping her to secure the arts and
science deanship that preceded her own time as provost. Now,
two years into the position, she needed to hear his views on several
subjects. While their long conversation was helpful on several
fronts, she really didn't like what he had to say about deans. What
it came down to, from his point of view, is that about one-third
of the deans he knew were exemplary, one-third were marginal
but adequate, and one-third were beyond redemption. He further
distressed her by insisting that some institutuions beat the odds
for awhile, but that over the long-haul the thirds will out. He
also told her that almost all problems were reducible to personnel
problems if you thought about them hard enough. What a dismal
view, she thought, and probably wrong. She wondered what she
would find if she asked a dozen provosts about the ratios. She
also wondered if many of them would be as honest with her about
it as her old mentor had been.

After several weeks of thinking about it, she listed a number
of options along with pros and cons as a way to move from thinking
toward some kind of action. After staring at her list for quite
awhile, Straight was amused that her Ph.D. in physical anthro-
pology, her years as a successful grant getter, her brief time as
chairperson, and her tenure as dean didn't seem to add much in

helping her to figure this one out. She didn't like any of the options. She knew that making one change wasn't going to solve
the whole problem. She also knew that unless that one change
was made, it would be very difficult to get on with making any
other changes. She could sense that the other deans were watching how she was going to handle this one. She didn't want to
miss the mark.

What options should be prominent on her list? How would
you advise her to proceed?

Response # 1

This is not an atypical situation for a new (or old) provost to be
in—finding that a predecessor did not leave a reasonably clean
table. Since accreditation is at stake and the need for curricular
reform is patent, the provost needs to act decisively. She needs
to show the other deans and the faculty that her resolve to improve
the overall quality of the academic programs is steadfast and that
to do so may require some stringent measures. Even though the
president appears not to be helpful, according to the scenario,
hopefully he or she is really supportive of the provost's mission.
I assume that in what follows.

Since the college of engineering doesn't have an administrative
evaluation process, I would suggest immediately establishing one.
The procedure I would proffer involves:

1. *Developing a "work plan."* Each of the deans and other
administrators reporting to the provost should prepare a draft
work plan for the ensuing academic year. The provost should pro10
an outline of the components to be addressed in the plan (e.g.,
long-range planning, curricular development, faculty development, affirmative action, fund-raising, community involvement).
This step will denote her expectations of what senior administrators
should be emphasizing—in this case, especially the dean of engineering. The draft plan should be reviewed by the provost, providing suggestions for modification (or addition), again reinforcing
her expectations of performance. The deans (and others) will then
revise their plans, with the aim of reaching agreement.

The provost will by this stage have indicated quite clearly what
she expects of the engineering dean and others. This step should

also trigger her senior officers, in turn to develop the same strategy for their subordinates. To be effective, this whole process should be initiated early enough to allow implementation beginning with the new academic year (or calendar year). Since it will be the first time, at least two months may be needed to conclude the process.

2. *Evaluation.* Since this is a new process, a rather informal formative evaluation session should be held in midyear, providing an opportunity for preliminary assessment of the degree to which goals are being met and for midcourse correction if that seems appropriate. This midyear evauation should be considered appropriate for any new dean or other senior administrator. At the end of the first year of implementation, and yearly thereafter, there should be a formal evaluation consisting of several components:

    a. A self-assessment prepared by the senior administrator addressing each component of the work plan.

    b. An appraisal of the senior administrator by one of more of the following: fellow deans/administrators, subordinate staff, faculty. However this is done, the results must be kept confidential to protect the individual making the assessment. Color coding the forms used would permit segregation of the categories of people sampled. Anonymity can be protected in a number of ways.

    c. An in-depth appraisal by the provost based on the two sources of input, including an interview and a written report for the personnel file. The deans should have an opportunity to review the penultimate version and submit suggestions for revision. The provost should reserve the right to accept or reject these suggestions in preparing the final version. The dean may file a rebuttal for the personnel file.

3. *Developing a new work plan.* The evaluation leads quite naturally to initiating a recycling of the process. Thus, it is a developmental process in which the provost can strengthen the performance of her people.

In the case in point, even at midyear the provost can inform the dean of engineering that all is not going well and that unless there is substantial improvement, she may find it necessary to request his resignation or terminate him. This would not come as a surprise unless everyone has been viewing the situation through rose-colored glasses. However—and importantly—this dean is not being singled out since all deans are being subjected to the same developmental evaluative process. Perhaps others will be found wanting on one or more fronts as well.

If, as seems likely, the dean of engineering will be found wanting, the provost must hang tough in her decision to fire him or seek his resignation. If she doesn't, her administrative integrity will be diminished and her overall effectiveness will wane. However, she must be fair, and a scheme such as this allows that to occur. She might also find some alternative but meaningful role the dean can play. He seems well-connected in the community, so perhaps some community relations post might be considered, a role in which he could save face and still contribute to the University. (Edward J. Kormondy, Chancellor, University of Hawaii-Hilo and West Oahu.)

Response # 2

This is a classic case in two senses. First, here is a well-entrenched, well-connected person whose long-standing reputation is not consistent with or applicable to present reality. Second, the case brings into bold relief academe's penchant for concentrating on personality and process rather than mission and objective. The result is—and this is emphasized by the old mentor's reaction—that an issue critical to the future of the university and to the university's obligation to its engineering students is treated as a personnel problem with its attendant human foibles.

While these classic considerations cannot be ignored, I would advise Provost Straight to set her sights clearly on the objectives—the modernization of the engineering curriculum, the development of faculty, and the achievement of accreditation. Then her options are clear and she is in a position to explain and, if necessary, defend her actions to those who are more concerned with Dean Prior's long service or the effects of his departure on a variety of actors. Moreover, she must be concerned about how others perceive her own job performance, especially the other deans.

I would advise Provost Straight to inform herself as to the

short- and long-term needs of the college of engineering and clarify in her own mind, from whatever internal or external sources are available to her—including, most definitely, confidential conversations with selected members of the engineering faculty—the direction the college must take. She should then hold a meeting with the dean in which she outlines her concepts and/or decisions regarding the future of the school and calls for the development of a five-year plan.

Further—and this is crucial—she must alert the dean to her concern, in view of his long service as dean, whether new leadership may be needed to develop and implement a long-range plan. She should make it clear that it is not because of a lack of appreciation for his work or a personality difference. Rather, it is a clear institutional need that she has personally identified—to plan in a longer time frame and to stimulate new initiatives in curriculum and faculty development. The dean should be asked to return in a week or so with his recommendations about how to proceed.

I surmise from what this case reveals about Dean Prior that he will want to go out with dignity. Whether that be via early retirement, terminal sabbatical, or return to the faculty—all with generous perks—can be determined. Should Dean Prior show no intention of discussing further the issue of new leadership, then Provost Straight must take on the unpleasant task of requesting his resignation as dean.

The old mentor's formula has a deceptive charm to it. Certainly, we can all think of dozens of situations in which personnel shifts make the difference. The cast that I would put on that, however, is that whether one's performance is exemplary, adequate, or beyond redemption is generally a matter of time and place. This may be why the longevity in top administrative posts is usually brief and why so many successful administrators tend to be mobile. The case of Dean Prior represents not a personnel problem but a failure of academic leadership in the past that the current provost has a chance to put straight. (Milton Greenberg, Provost and Vice President for Academic Affairs, The American University, Washington, D.C.)

Response # 3

This problem is a particularly difficult one for a provost. The fact that Provost Straight is new to her appointment gives her some opportunities that may have been barred to her predecessor, but of course there are risks as well. Examining the available options is a useful way to begin.

Option 1: Do nothing

Rather than taking the initiative, the provost can simply wait until further developments create a stronger base for action. For example, the failure of the college to receive accreditation can hardly fail to have been noted by faculty and community. If matters are as bad as the provost suspects, accreditation will be denied again. Although denial of accreditation is undesirable, the new provost can hardly be blamed for it, and in any case there is little she can do to bring about the necessary changes in curriculum in time to affect the outcome. Another denial of accreditation might be the catalyst producing a demand that something be done. At that point she may be in a stronger position to bring about a change of leadership in the college.

Option 2: Work with the dean to bring about change

The description of the dean contains interesting contradictions. Although he gives the impression of lack of vitality, the history of the college indicates that for a long time the dean exercised effective leadership and was able to persuade the provost's predecessor to give the college additional resources. In spite of his apparent lack of vitality, he seems vigorous enough when taking a stand against early retirement. So there seems to be some latent reserve of energy to be tapped. The provost might learn from the dean and others about issues that the dean has had to confront and on which he needs her help. Perhaps the attitude of the entrenched senior faculty is as much a problem to the dean as to the provost. She might try to establish herself as the dean's ally in bringing about change.

Option 3: Work on the dean to persuade him to step down

Although the dean probably knows he is out of favor with the administration, he is apparently resisting change and does not want to step down. Yet the impression he gives of lack of vitality suggests that he is no longer enjoying his work. In a series of one-on-one talks, the provost might be able to bring the discussion around to the point where the dean himself mentions that he is weary of the continuing efforts to serve as the college's advocate in an unfavorable climate. The provost might be able to give the

dean an image of himself as a successful but embattled leader
who has done as much as can be expected and who has paid his
dues. When the dean can view stepping down as something other
than failure, retirement may begin to look more attractive.

Option 4: Request the dean's resignation

The simplest and most forthright approach might be to let the
dean know he is finished. Although there may be opposition from
some sources, it is also possible that the provost may receive high
marks for taking hold of a difficult situation in a courageous manner. The deans who are watching her to see what she will do
might just applaud her action, especially since they were apparently irritated when the college of engineering received more
support from her predecessor than the college seems to have de-
served. If she can combine this action with a well-publicized plan
to recruit a new dean with outstanding credentials and record of
accomplishments, she may get much internal and external support
for her bold action.

How to Proceed?

The provost should give option 2 a good try. Without spending
more time on the approach than can be spared, she can test the
possibilities of helping the dean to bring about desired changes.
If the college is again denied accreditation, as seems likely, she
can use this outcome as a starting point for her efforts to involve
the dean in advancing the college's interests. During this period
she should do everything possible to let it be widely known that
she is working with the dean to bring about change. If after a
reasonable effort she is convinced that the dean cannot provide
the leadership she requires, option 3 should be tried. If the dean
shows no signs of interest in stepping down, the provost should
use option 4. In fact, she should consider whether the situation
is urgent enough to ask for the dean's resignation as soon as it
becomes clear that option 2 has failed.

Working on option 2 is important because as a new provost she
needs some time to establish herself as an administrator who has
the best interests of her institution in mind, whatever she does.
She also needs time to assess the situation thoroughly to see where
her support will come from. However, she must not allow the
matter to drift without action, and above all she must manage to

convey to interested parties that she is actively pursuing a satisfactory resolution of the problem. (Norma S. Rees, Vice Chancellor
for Academic Affairs, University of Wisconsin-Milwaukee.)

Each of the responses to this case study suggests the need for
the provost to take action—to *do* something—reasonably quickly
as well as decisively. Others in the university community are
watching closely. A successful dean or provost must know when
something can be postponed, when it can be forgotten, and when
it must be immediately addressed.

The first response (Chancellor Kormondy) stresses the need
for systematic planning and evaluation procedures and suggests
how a version of the growth contract can be an excellent communications device to all deans and other administrators reporting
to the provost. The second response (Provost Greenberg) goes
more directly to the case in point. The solution here is to refocus
on mission and objectives and treat the problem of the dean as a
consequence. The third response (Vice Chancellor Rees) enum-
erates available options and argues for an initial, well-publicized
but carefully limited development effort with a planned series of
escalations if early attempts do not succeed. All three responses
indicate that this is a matter requiring considerable thought on
the part of the provost. Replacing a dean is not a small piece of
business.

Facing a Censure Vote

One of the more negative dimensions of academic leadership is
the potential it provides for others to be truly hurtful, whether
intentionally or not. This actually occurred in the following case
study.

CASE STUDY

Academic Vice President Charlie Flint was clearly apprehensive
about the phone call he knew was coming. He had just finished
a not altogether satisfactory session with the arts and sciences

dean to plan yet another year's faculty and staff reductions. The enrollment started to drop three years ago, and in spite of several ingenious position-saving moves, faculty and staff cuts had to be deeper and deeper each year. Now, with a state fiscal crisis joining forces with enrollment declines, he knew that reductions would have to go much further into the ranks of tenured faculty.

For several years now, Flint and his aides had pumped out a continuous flow of information about the university's worsening situation. Planning committees had been convened with faculty, administration, and staff representation and participation. By and large they had worked well, and the cuts that were announced after thorough discussion were widely seen as fair. Even so, Flint knew that the faculty couldn't sit still for the release of tenured members. He had heard from several quarters that the faculty senate was anticipating a censure vote. Even though the entire administration was to be censured, Flint knew that, as the man in charge of the reductions, he was the primary target of the vote.

The chair of the faculty senate was a fairly solid faculty member. He had a good reputation for his teaching and had done a modest but acceptable amount of research. All of this was only secondary to the fact that he was a consummate campus politician. With him, nothing was ever quite what it seemed at the outset. If he was involved in a censure vote, it was clear that there was more to it than yielding to his constituency's need to slap someone's wrist. He had been helpful all along in making sure that the senate sent its best people to participate in the planning process. Now he was about to lead the charge to censure the result.

These musings ended when the phone started to ring. Sure enough, it was the senate president informing Flint that a special senate meeting was being convened to consider a censure vote. The senate executive committee had decided that "fair is fair" and that the president, academic vice president, and financial affairs vice president should be invited to address the senate before any censure resolution was introduced. The president, of course, would be out of town (again) and the financial affairs vice president told them that he really had nothing to say beyond the several detailed budget memos he had prepared and released. He indicated that he didn't believe it woud serve anyone's ends for him to appear and rehash what everybody already painfully knew. That left Flint.

Should Flint accept the invitation, and, if so, what should be his strategy for addressing the senate?

Response # 1

In actuality, the vice president for academic affairs functions as a buffer between the administration and the faculty. Keeping in mind the concept of a buffer, one will readily understand that the person in such a position will feel the *shock and pressure* from both administrators and faculty. If the chief academic officer is fortunate enough to work with other administrators who understand the relationship of quality academic programs to the prestige and future of the academy, there is less likelihood that the faculty will view reductions in resources and personnel as an administrative tactic geared to keep the faculty in line. On the other hand, if the corporate management style is transferred in its entirety from the business world to the academy without understanding the basic differences between business institutions and institutions of higher education, there is a strong possibility that the faculty will have the perception that *quality* of the instructional program is of less importance than *quantity* (that is, enrollment increases in spite of quality).

The mere suggestion on the part of the administration that tenured faculty are to be eliminated implies that the university has reached the point where those who have distinguished themselves through exemplary teaching, research, and other outstanding services are no longer needed. Hence, the vice president of academic affairs is faced with determining if the administration views the cause of academic excellence and the quality of graduates of the institution as a primary concern. Rightly or wrongly, tenured faculty feel that they make a significant difference in the quality of life and programs at institutions of higher education. Considering the resulting emotionalism engendered when there is the slightest hint that the administration is becoming overly involved in the tenure process, it is likely that the faculty will strike out in some way. If not censure, there will be some form of negativeness toward central administration. Those at the top of the academic pyramid must be prepared to accept such a response as an occupational hazard. A vice president finding himself or herself in such a position would do well to recognize his or her role as buffer, put on a bullet proof vest, and meet the faculty with sincerity, candor, integrity, and compassion. The chief academic officer, being in a key position, must strive to be fair, but strong and decisive, when critical decisions are to be made. The monologue that follows is intended to convey the message that the administration is concerned, but in putting forth every effort to save the university it is forced to take the drastic measure of releasing some tenured faculty.

Vice President for Academic Affairs' Speech to the Faculty

Reduction of tenured faculty is perhaps one of the most drastic measures and emotionally traumatic events that can occur within the academic community. Historically, faculty have striven for tenure through the demonstration of excellence in teaching. They have distinguished themselves in research and creative pursuits and have provided exemplary service to students, the university, and the broader community. The faculty here at Seashore University is no exception. As vice president for academic affairs, I have been privileged to work with the promotion and tenure committee. I have reviewed your dossiers and numerous professional accomplishments. There is no doubt that the greatness of this university has been built on the pursuit of excellence in teaching, research, and service.

On a personal note, as one who has come through the ranks I know full well the diligence and perserverance required in the pursuit of tenure. As a young professional, I remember well the feeling of exhilaration when I was informed that I had won the coveted award—that is, I had been granted tenure. Here, as in all institutions of higher education, the acquisition of tenure has long been a mark of distinction and has given professionals a sense of security.

Colleagues, we are living at a time when there are few, if any, universals. The nation and the world are in a fluid state. The security that once came with acquiring a formal education, to say nothing of a terminal degree, is no longer with us. The changes in supply and demand in the Information Age have just begun to affect higher education. There are many demographics that affect the demand for a number of the programs offered by institutions of higher education.

First and foremost, there is a decline in the number of college age students among middle and upper socioeconomic groups. Second, although higher education continues to be the most direct route to economic success for lower class and minority groups, the escalating costs of education often make such a dream unrealistic.

Third, the high technology of the Information Society has not only reduced the demand for workers at the lower end of the spectrum, but has also lessened the demand for university-trained personnel in corporate America.

Fourth, colleges and universities, with their traditional method of offering courses and degrees, are being challenged by others who have entered the educational marketplace. A number of major industries as well as governmental agencies are providing on-the-job training for employees, utilizing professors from universities such as ours to provide instruction in degree and nondegree programs.

Finally, as a result of the electronic boom, it is now possible to offer instruction in nontraditional modes. We have yet to realize the full impact of satellites, videos, and computers on the enrollment of college students in courses at universities such as ours.

I do not wish to imply that the downtrend in enrollment at this institution is the result of any single factor. However, we do know that we have lost students, in spite of our best efforts. We have reached the point where we must accept the strong possibility that we will have to take drastic measures to find a way to absorb those losses through a reduction in faculty.

You are gathered here to protest and condemn such action. I share your concern about the future of the university. I also share your concern about the possibility of further reductions of faculty. You may be assured that the administration is not arbitrarily trying to get rid of faculty. We have reduced noninstructional and support staff. We have instituted cost-saving strategies in auxiliary services.

During the past three years I have watched the steady decline in enrollment. We have now reached the point we all feared. We must consider further reduction in faculty, including some with tenure. Colleagues, the fact remains that you must have students in order to provide the diverse programs that are reflected in the catalogues of this institution. We simply have more instructors, including some with tenure, than we can support with the current student enrollment.

As we meet the crisis, we will attempt to assist you in finding other positions. We will identify the areas of greatest demand at this university to see if there might be some matching of talent. We will also be available to meet with you on an individual basis to determine how we may be of assistance during this professional crisis.

I wish I could give you a different message. However, you should know that the administration is indebted to you for your commitment to excellence in spite of adversity. We understand your concern, and pledge to continue to work to preserve the rights of the faculty and students within the means available.

I appreciate the opportunity you have given me to address you. I look forward to the future with optimism. (Martha E. Dawson, Vice President for Academic Affairs, Hampton University, Hampton, Virginia.)

Response # 2

Charlie Flint has been an academic vice president too long to think that one can play that role and avoid being called every variation of the word bastard, whatever one does. So that's no factor in the decision confronting him in the telephone call from the faculty senate's chair. Flint knows that there is another label he cannot afford—Charlie the Wimp. So he seizes the moment and lets the senate chair know that he expected and welcomes the invitation, that he'll plan to present a statement, and that he'll take "an additional quarter hour or so" to field questions from the senators. Hanging up the telephone, he thinks ruefully how much time one has to deal with insignificant matters, but how quickly one must react to issues affecting one's survival. "Trust the gut" has long been one of Charlie Flint's mottoes; another is, "Life is absurd."

Now to questions of strategy. Delaying the meeting is moot; the time was already established when the senate chair called Charlie. That frees him from scrambling to get very much new information together to illustrate his points. There are some old transparencies from the planning committee's sessions and they'll make good stage props, background for his one-person theatrical performance. (The solo rendition of a work intended for three actors will not go unnoticed by the faculty. Flint ought not refer to the situation. His single chair will say more than the empty chairs at the debates to which political incumbents are invited by their challengers.) His appearance should be entitled "Terse eloquence."

So Flint seizes his moment. Act I—he admits head on that an appearance in the climate of charges of censure is tough, but that he sees this as one of those opportunities for the academic leadership the faculty deserves and that he is dedicated to providing. "Would any of them, placed in his position, do it differently?", he asks, looking them in the eye. "Would they have respected him had he declined to walk to the front of the room?" A reference to the burden he and the senate's chair carry ends the act.

Act II—he takes five minutes to sketch a vision for the institution, the ways he wishes it to look different ten years from now. Each of those dreams, he notes, will require some painful decisions, some alteration of the mission that served the institution so well when the generations most represented in the senate began teaching, reminding them of the tradeoffs that made possible their places in that faculty. Let them hear the academic vice president speak of the honors college, the wellness center, the graduation requirement in ethics and values.

Act III begins with Flint at the overhead projector, pointer at the columns of projections and the trend curves. He reminds them that these are the data designed and used by their joint committee over these past years. He never wavers from using the term "painful reality," from warning them of dangers not unknown in academic institutions when leaders put their heads in the sand. A similar university just across the state line—the one that did no planning and found itself forced to release many of its promising untenured faculty—is a good case study to mention. Throughout Act III there is the refrain, "The governor, the legislature, the higher education commission will move in on us if we do not make our decisions. And so we must continue collegially but quickly and without disruption of the process that has served us so well."

Act IV is very short, by design and by the constraint of a tight script that allows twenty minutes for the entire play. Now Charlie has another rhetoric than that of vision or reality. He invokes analogies to warfare, to the escalation of weaponry, to military madness. Censure, he not untenderly reminds the audience, is one of the faculty's near-ultimate weapons. What, he asks, is left after that bomb has gone off? That reminder to a group engaged in its own political campaigns against nuclear proliferation might drive home. And then Act IV, Scene II, the prelude to the curtain and crucial curtain call. This is Charlie Flint at his best, the person who will in the future, as in the past, share decision-making with the faculty's own leaders.

Encores in faculty senate meetings are not measured by applause but by the tenor of the questions. Now Charlie takes risks, for he has saved some good ammunition for this. He needs questions that permit him to fire off a shot of great importance to the battle. Somehow he must respond to the senate about the purpose of tenure. It will require knowledge of American Association of University Professors (AAUP) language, of Hofstader on academic freedom in America, of the struggles for preservation of freedom of speech in the classroom and in research. That, not job security, Flint must say, is the fundamental rationale for tenure. If no one— Flint or the faculty—has absolute security of job, the protection each side needs is that of a fair process for decision-making. With that, and with the confident stride of a Reagan leaving the press conference, Flint departs to deal with pressing university business.

Postscript. Charlie Flint will know the weight of a threatened censure vote. Such things are commonplace on some campuses and they have the same impact as that of the boy "who cried wolf" too often. I sense that to be the case here or I'd guess the president would jolly well cancel his other obligations. (David Johnson, Dean of the College, Gustavus-Adolphus College, St. Peter., Minnesota.)

Both of these responses make it clear that the invitation must be accepted. While there is a considerable difference in the proposed nature of the remarks to be made at the senate meeting, both responses contain useful ideas for a dean or provost anticipating the need to make such a presentation. The first response (Vice President Dawson) appeals directly to the values academics hold dear. The theatrical metaphor in the second response (Dean Johnson) reminds us that the presentation, after all, is in fact a performance. It needs to be a good one. While a twenty-minute speech might or might not turn a potential censure vote around, it can earn many credits for the performer if it is well done. Those credits may well be quite useful in whatever lies ahead.

Independent of the particular response one makes to this situation, the provost or dean must be prepared for emotion and unreason from the faculty. To a degree often surprising to an outsider, the academy can display emotions in direct conflict with the measured application of reason it trumpets in defense of its mission and academic freedom. The trick for the academic officer is to recognize and prepare for such occasional unreason without falling into cynicism.

The Athletic Director and the Provost

Trying to satisfy several constituencies simultaneously can be, quite literally, impossible. Difficulties are almost guaranteed when there are revenue shortfalls and program reduction is in the offing. Decisions can be further complicated when friendships are involved, as the following case illustrates.

CASE STUDY

The AD shifted nervously in his chair in the provost's outer office. His relations with the provost had been pleasant and useful since he came to State two years ago. Now, the coaches were quite upset, the booster club regulars were livid, and he was the man in the middle.

Things had been going well. Most of the teams were doing better than they had in the past, facilities and transportation were being upgraded for women's teams in keeping with the university's rigorous affirmative action program, and the recruiting of good athletes was proceeding nicely. This was not the time for a major budget reversal; yet, that was what he faced.

The provost had called for a $50,000 reduction in the athletic budget for next year. A drop in enrollment coincided with a fiscal problem in the state, and the governor and legislature mandated budget reductions in all units of state government. Universities, like everyone else, had to make reductions. The AD knew that except for good press and favorable relations with the president and provost, athletics' share of the reduction might be even larger, but he was unable to convince his people of that.

The athletic advisory committee, dominated by faculty and students, recommended across-the-board cuts in all athletic programs. The boosters recommended dropping the least lucrative sport. The coaches recommended dropping as many nonrevenue sports as it took to make the budget reduction and temporarily reassigning their coaches to PE instruction. The AD knew that each of these recommendations could not be lived with. Doing the first two would change their NCAA status, and the third was clearly impossible because HPER was overstaffed already. Since sizable faculty cuts were also being made, the AD knew that seeking to add personnel to HPER was untenable.

Provost Jim Johnson, himself an athletic booster, had heard of the AD's difficulty from several sources. He also heard that the AD was going to reject all recommendations he had received and propose instead to make up the money through a more extensive advanced season ticket sale than they had ever tried before. The president correctly saw this as "betting on the come" and was not likely to support it.

Since Provost Johnson was an old friend of the AD and had helped recruit him for the institution, he, too, felt himself to be on the spot. Here was his friend in the outer office to ask for help, support, and advice.

What kind of advice should Provost Johnson give the AD?

Response # 1

The friendship and mentor relationship between Provost Johnson and the AD are helpful, but the response should be the same as if there were no such relationship. The occasion of a reduction in budget—and in program—is one calling for good planning and a look at priorities in the athletics programs, even though the time available for them is short. None of the solutions proposed is an appropriate response.

Cutting across-the-board is an abdication of managerial and leadership responsibility. Such an approach was not and is not taken in buiding up programs and deserves to be discarded for the reverse process, in spite of its apparent attraction as being fair and equitable. It is neither. Equal percentage or equal dollar cuts in different programs are unrelated to the impact on those programs: In some cases the effect could be severe; in others, very minor. And this approach short-changes the institution most of all, since the institutional priorities are not considered.

Using the level of production of revenue by a program as the sole criterion for cuts is also a short-sighted approach that probably does not meet institutional goals. The modification proposed by the coaches to drop nonrevenue sports and reassign the coaches to physical education shows a remarkable lack of understanding of such a step, or perhaps a suspicion of the cutting process, since it should have been made clear that all were being reviewed for cuts. If this were understood, then it is just an attempt to transfer the problem from the athletics program to the physical education program. Somewhere, the $50,000 will still have to be found.

The proposal of the AD to push for more revenue is a "wish" solution that is not responsible budgetarily. If more revenue were to be available through greater sales of advanced tickets, there would still be no assurance that the total over the year would increase, nor that the increase was sustainable over a longer period. In proposing such a solution, the AD may be indicating his or her view of the gravity of the situation. If the suggestion is made, it should give Provost Johnson concern that the AD was panicking.

The provost should point out to the AD that the situation called for (1) an analysis of the priorities of the university's althletic programs, as judged by the AD and the community; (2) a decision to eliminate or drastically reduce one or more programs judged to be least productive for the university at this time; and (3) strenuous efforts to increase revenue. This process calls for communication and cooperation with the appropriate advisers (faculty, students, and active alumni), but the responsibility for the decisions has to rest with the AD. Notwithstanding the possibility of increased revenue, the reductions should meet the $50,000 target.

The process of assessing programs and their relative importance to the university should provide strength to the athletics programs in the future. In addition to pointing out where reductions could be made, it would provide guidance to where increases could do the most good. Provost Johnson should point out that the athletics programs of future years could actually benefit from this process. It is often very difficult to reduce or eliminate less-successful programs when there is no forced mandate to do so. In the current situation, the external pressures to reduce programs could provide a means of strengthening the athletics department in the future. (Maurice Glicksman, Provost and Dean of Faculty, Brown University, Providence, Rhode Island.)

Response # 2

There are occasions when a difficult problem can be converted into a "management opportunity" for the creative administrator. This particular scenario could easily fall into that category. The provost should seize this opportunity to assert greater control over the athletic department—something that most knowledgeable observers of intercollegiate athletics believe needs to be accomplished nationwide.

The provost might suggest that the time has come to review the entire program in athletics. Title IX commitments need to be carefully considered. Levels of competition need to be realistically set. The often treacherous waters surrounding booster club fund-raising needs to be examined and the long-term potential for ticket sales assessed. A plan needs to be developed that not only incorporates the $50,000 reduction in budget but assesses priorities, sets goals, and places them into a budgetary context. Such a plan, of course, would require approval by the provost and the president. Within this mechanism, various administrative concerns could be addressed.

If the AD is typical of his or her peers from around the nation, long-term planning is not part of his modus operandi. Only a few institutions in the United States can compete nationally in all individual sports, but most athletic departments do not recognize that reality in their budgeting. Budget constraints simply prohibit such a level of competition, except for the Notre Dames and UCLAs of major college athletics. The provost might therefore request that this long-range plan include the placement of each men's and women's sport into one of three categories:

1. Those few programs that will be budgeted at a level to achieve national recognition (these will probably include the revenue-generating sports such as basketball and football).

2. Those sports that will be budgeted to sustain championship-level competition within the conference.

3. Those sports that will be supported at a minimum level to encourage participation but with little expectation of winning championships.

Such a plan would enable the AD to allocate the budget on a systematic basis while providing the provost and president with an opportunity to participate in setting institutional athletic goals.

Assuming that the institution in question is competing at a Division I-A NCAA level, the $50,000 cut would probably amount to less than 2 percent of the annual athletic budget. Such a cut could readily be absorbed by a variety of solutions:

1. Reducing travel and recruitment costs across-the-board in all sports.

2. Reducing other operating costs across-the-board.

3. Freezing an existing vacancy or two in assistant coaching positions (men's basketball and football are eminently qualified for such reductions at most Division I-A institutions).

The provost might also ask impertinent questions such as the following to prod the AD into taking one of the above courses:

1. Are eight assistant football coaches absolutely necessary?

2. Do you need two full-time men's assistant basketball coaches in addition to two graduate assistants?

3. Is the football team's "extra" twelfth game in Hawaii necessary?

4. Must you fill all ninety-five authorized football scholarships when less than fifty players ever play a significant role during a season? (A reduction of ten such scholarships will probably meet the entire deficit.)

5. Are all the associate and assistant athletic directors really necessary?

6. Can we use last year's uniforms another year?

Finally, the provost must emphasize that the $50,000 cut is part of a university-wide activity and athletics must do its share.

The provost should observe that he has already been bloodied by angry faculty, irate deans, and enraged department chairs who have much less flexibility in cutting their budgets than does the athletic department. In fact, it would be a grievous error for the athletic department not to participate in the cut. The exigencies of campus politics dictate that athletics not receive favored treatment ahead of academic programs.

If the provost can handle this conference with his friend adeptly, the new AD will leave the administration building much happier than when he arrived. (Richard O. Davies, Vice President for Academic Affairs, University of Nevada-Reno.)

Response # 3

Provost Johnson must give strong and clear advice to his AD. Most importantly, the credibility and validity of the state and university budget process must be maintained. Therefore, the first item on the agenda must be the willingness of the provost to meet with the athletic advisory committee, the booster club, and the coaches to explain the extent of the budget reduction for the entire campus and to document that athletics' share of the reduction could very well have been larger. At each of these meetings, the ability to answer all questions with clear, reasonable, fair, and respectful responses is critical for maintaining the credibility of the process.

Once the validity of the reduction has been established, the provost can advise the AD on how to proceed. The general principle to follow is to do what is "least harmful" to the athletic program and the institution. Applying this principle, however, is not easy; to most people, least harmful means that someone else's budget will be cut. Here is where the responsibility and good judgment of the AD is given a major test. The recommendations of various advisory groups and persons must be given careful, fair, and thorough review, and the AD must identify budget reductions that can be respected by his or her colleagues and the administration.

If the current allocation of resources to each sport is appropriate and equitable—based on the number and quality of athletes and coaches, fan support, and operating costs—an across-the-board cut may make the most sense and produce minimal harm for everyone. If, as the AD alleges, this would result in a change in NCAA status, then some sports must already be operating at a survival margin, where even a minimal reduction would force their elimination. It is apparent that the AD does not want to make any reduction that would force a change in NCAA status. This is a policy decision that should be reviewed by university administration, either affirming or changing the policy. Questions about NCAA status need to be discussed with boosters and coaches as well, since the recommendations of these groups could force such a change. The number of men's and women's sports for a given NCAA status may very well draw the boundaries for the budget reduction and automatically eliminate certain options. Participation in a given athletic conference may also affect these decisions.

If the university decides to retain all sports, the selective pruning of all available resources must begin. Are there any vacant positions, either full- or part-time, that can be sacrificed? Are there any approaching retirements or resignations where the position could be filled at a lower salary? Are any selective reductions possible in recruiting, travel, advertising, publications, etc?

Trying to offset reductions with an increase in season ticket sales is probably unwise. Unless the increase is substantial and can be maintained in future years, it would not solve the problem permanently. It is better to use increases in revenue to support enhancements in quality rather than basic, ongoing budget requirements.

Timing is very important. Deciding too quickly usually implies less careful analysis and often means little or no consultation. Prolonging the cutting process usually implies lack of decisiveness by administrators and often means longer periods of stress for areas that are not likely to be cut. Finding the optimum time is difficult but essential.

Although many persons and groups have already participated in the process by recommending various actions, it is also wise to invite them to comment on the AD's recommendations to the provost. If the AD can document least harm from adopting his proposals, the respect for his or her stewardship should continue. The provost's support for these recommendations is then absolutely necessary. The AD is in the middle and must work effectively with upper administration, faculty, coaches, students, and boosters. A talented person can do the job well. (Otto F. Bauer, Vice Chancellor for Academic Affairs, University of Nebraska-Omaha.)

The responses all call for planning and consultation followed by action. The first response (Provost Glicksman) calls for involvement of the AD in the university's long-range planning process. While such processes usually deal mainly with deans, chairs, and academic departments, it is a wise provost who has extended the scope of such processes to include the AD, registrar, library, academic computer center, and other areas reporting to the provost. The second response (Vice President Davies) highlights the need to establish and review priorities as an integral part of the planning process. The third response (Vice Chancellor Bauer) suggests a round of discussions between the provost and relevant committees and groups before anything else happens.

It is clear in all three responses that a provost cannot expect merely to announce reduction targets and then sit back and wait for the detailed results to roll in. Many of the people reporting to the provost will need help in dealing effectively with reduction targets. Until the results are in and agreed to, the provost will have to deal with the problems that arise on a day-to-day basis, even if those days are already filled with other important business.

Whither Goeth Continuing Education?

Continuing education divisions have become increasingly important, both as modes of campus outreach and as sources of revenue. As this trend has developed, continuing education divisions have also become larger, more highly bureaucratized, and surrounded by regulations. One of the consequences of this increased structural and procedural red tape is often a loss of entrepreneurial spirit and higher costs for the services rendered. As these factors become apparent, other units of the university, particularly in business and/or engineering colleges, take the initiative and offer continuing education programs of their own.

These programs may violate institutional understandings regarding tuition to be charged, effect on faculty load, availability of equipment for off-campus instruction, and a host of other variables. If the institution seeks to require that all continuing education activities be conducted through the continuing education division, it tends to stifle outreach and creativity in the colleges. If, on the other hand, it lets the colleges each go their own way, an unacceptably wide variety of practices will ensue, and the effectiveness of the continuing education division will be diminished.

Central to the conflicts that can emerge are questions of who gets to keep the revenue generated and where the credit hours are to be tallied. To what extent must continuing education revenue produced in the colleges underwrite the university's general cost of doing business? Do these funds supplement university general fund allocations to the colleges or in some measure replace them? When departmental credit-hour productivity is being analyzed, should continuing education credit hours be reckoned separately or merged with the credit hours produced by regular on-campus instruction? Deans and provosts need to be mindful of one another's concerns as these matters arise.

CASE STUDY

Jim Everready had been dean of continuing education for seven years. They were good years, and he had been able to build an effective instructional outreach program for the university. He took considerable comfort during all that development from the steady support of the recently retired provost. Together they had been able to shepherd a set of procedural guidelines and regulations through the faculty senate, and the faculty seemed quite pleased with the way the continuing education mission of the university was being handled.

Recently, however, it all seemed to be unraveling. Whether it was the arrival of a new provost that prompted the deans of the colleges to develop their own continuing education operations or the pressure of the times, Dean Everready couldn't really tell. The new provost, William Cranston, had clearly run on a platform of decentralization and local control in winning the provost's job over several other significant candidates. Coming from the outside, Cranston would have little knowledge of how the system had been built and perhaps little appreciation of how it was now deteriorating.

The problem was that the deans of the colleges of engineering and business were operating as free agents, paying little attention to the rules that had been established, running in to offer selected courses rather than articulated programs, picking off the best part of the market and ignoring the rest, and paying little heed to quality control. Everready had heard recently on the grapevine that the deans were sending out some pretty marginal people as instructors and were toying with a variety of pricing structures. As if this wasn't bad enough, they had taken to advertising their wares in the local media as if a continuing education division didn't exist.

From Everready's perspective, it looked like the other deans were going to have to be reined in, brought into compliance with university policy, and preferably constrained to developing their initiatives in cooperation with the division of continuing education. He didn't know, however, how a new provost was going to corral two strong deans, especially when that new provost was an advocate of decentralization.

As Cranston stepped from his office with a warm smile and extended hand, Everready still wasn't sure what approach to take. In the old days he would have dealt with the other deans himself. Now he wasn't sure that would be productive.

How would you advise Everready?

Response # 1

Since the locus of control and an institution's philosophy regarding continuing education (and many other programs) seem to change over time, the best approach for a service provider is to be prepared to adapt to change. The hallmark of those who stay in these types of positions is that they are willing to adjust to differing philosophies and the changing needs of the various academic deans and department chairpersons. The key to survival is maintaining the quality of the products and services of the service unit—in this case continuing education—knowing that there always will be a demand for quality work well done, if the price is right.

Sometimes it takes a while for the present and prospective students to express themselves, but if an integrated curriculum is not provided, the provost will very soon be aware of the changes in enrollment and be able to understand and make adjustments in the offerings of the institution.

For the moment, Everready could ask Cranston to name a

committee to develop a policy on the continuing education function through which Everready could potentially cause the institution to join the issue in a more rational manner than a sheer power struggle would typically allow. Of course, this advice is very rational and if Everready has a hidden agenda related perhaps to a need for personal control rather than a desire to serve, he may need different advice.

The most successful deans of continuing education work cooperatively with the deans of the individual schools and colleges and attempt to provide only those services that the continuing education division can provide at a higher quality and a lower cost than the deans of the schools and colleges can provide. Specialization of labor still governs as one of the most successful means of coping with a relatively free market system. In the end, the dean of continuing education must be a team player—supportive of the other academic officers. (Raymond M. Haas, Vice President for Administration, University of Virginia, Charlottesville, Virginia.)

Response # 2

Jim Everready's position as dean of continuing education and the guidelines/regulations that he had been able to shepherd through the faculty senate are being seriously threatened. It's apparent that the deans of engineering and business are capitalizing on the new provost's views on decentralization and local control. However, both deans must be feeling pressure from their faculties to promote income opportunities. By going outside the continuing education unit, these opportunities were probably easier to obtain and available on a more selective basis than would be possible through the continuing education unit, which by nature has a broader mission and a broader university responsibility.

Questionable quality, a lack of articulated program direction, the use of marginal people as instructors, variation in price structures, and decentralized marketing all threaten the reputation of continuing education and the university as well as the schools of business and engineering. Dean Everready faces a difficult task in persuading Provost Cranston that decentralization in the continuing education area will result in a weakened position for the university. However, Everready has a responsibility to return these two schools to the guidelines and regulations passed by the faculty.

Dean Everready's first points with the provost should clarify that the continuing education unit strongly supports entrepreneurial activity and recognizes that the schools of business and engineering have excellent opportunities to develop new programs in support of the university's continuing education efforts. Referring to the lack of direction, quality problems, variation in pricing, etc., Dean Everready must convince Provost Cranston of the need for quality control and also that the continuing education unit has been able to maintain quality and programmatic direction over the last several years in accordance with the guidelines and procedures accepted by the university community.

It is important that Dean Everready make the provost aware of the continuing education unit's willingness to be especially aware of quickly developing opportunities for the business and engineering faculties. However, it should be stressed that these opportunities must be curricularly sound and programmatically aligned with the mission of the department, the school, and the university. Dean Everready must also emphasize his need to have high visibility/high demand programs such as business and engineering *in the continuing education program*. These areas draw students who eventually choose or recommend study beyond business and engineeering courses/updates. When the continuing education unit packages its programs appropriately or offers such courses/updates in conjunction with off-campus programming efforts, other areas of the university benefit as well.

The question of the individual's mission—what activities the faculty members wish to be involved in—and the institutional mission—what the university feels it is responsible to provide to its public—is at the heart of the conflict. In a good continuing education program, like the one developed by Jim Everready and the former provost, the following are considered: the goals and mission of the individual academic units, and the goals of the faculty. The entrepreneurial efforts of the schools of business and enigineering address the individual goals of the faculty without consideration for the programmatic goals of the university. Dean Everready needs to remind the provost that "marginal" individuals are not delivering their educational programs on the basis of their well-established reputations but rather on the strength of their affiliation with the university and their respective schools.

Dean Everready should level with the new provost and explain that before Provost Cranston's emphasis on decentralization and local control he (Everready) would have approached these two deans as the dean of continuing education and would have asked that the activities promoted by their schools be presented in compliance with university policy and in cooperation with continuing eduation. Dean Everready should explain his reasons— including quality control, programmatic consistency, adherence to the university mission, etc.—for wanting to centralize these activities. He should seek the provost's support in establishing a dialogue with the deans of engineering and business. Compliance with the regulations, involvement of the continuing education office in developing and presenting programs and, finally, a clarification of the willingness of the continuing education office to continue to support the entrepreneurial efforts of the business and engineering faculties within the programmatic guidelines of the university would be among the appropriate outcomes of these discussions. (Jack Oblak, Dean of Humanities and Sciences, Ithaca College, Ithaca, New York.)

These two quite different responses reflect the ongoing tension between continuing education and other academic units on many campuses. The first response (Vice President Haas) recommends the establishment of a committee to take a fresh look at the guidelines and stresses the importance of effective cooperation between the deans of continuing education and those of engineering and business. The second response (Dean Oblak) points out that the continuing education division has broader responsibilities than those of individual schools and colleges. His response is based on the fact that guidelines have been in place for some time and were working reasonably well before the decentralization emphasis came about. It is clear in both responses that the parties involved need to talk and listen to one another. Provost Cranston would be wise not to allow himself to be maneuvered into deciding the issue. Pushing problems back down to the deans may be among the most important work a provost does.

CHAPTER THREE

Maintaining Balance In the Academic Enterprise

THE CASE STUDIES in this chapter deal with shifting emphases and the problems that arise from seeking to maintain or redirect the balance of the academic enterprise. Shifting student interests, together with the current pronounced trend toward vocationalism, provide a variety of challenges. Imbalances between the supply of faculty expertise and the areas of student demand are among the most difficult of these challenges.

Curricular integrity requires at some point that lines be drawn and that the marketplace of student interest not become the sole criterion in the staffing of academic offerings and degree programs. The academic enterprise can become seriously misdirected where this occurs. Maintaining a balance appropriate to the mission of the institution, the expertise of the faculty, and the interests of the students is an important academic leadership responsibility. If the students don't see the value of what they're learning, they'll go somewhere else. If the institution leans too far toward vocational interests, the students may not get a good education. It isn't a question of either/or. It's a matter of balance. Deans and provosts should be proactive participants in seeing to it that the best possible balance is struck.

Preserving an Essential Department

The following case study illustrates the impact of shifting student interest upon a traditional academic offering. The more liberal academic offerings too often suffer student neglect as job procurement motivations come to the fore. The plight of history is shared by philosophy, religious studies, the fine arts, and most foreign languages. Maintaining strength in these areas requires adjustments of curriculum and staffing. At the same time, decisions about "essential" activities must be firmly rooted in the mission of the institution. Each institution must find its own balance, and the deans and provost must help it to do so.

CASE STUDY

Dean Graves sat for some time, staring at the blank pad on his work table at home. He had been invited by the history faculty and chairperson to come to their next department meeting to discuss the future of the department. Although he had plenty of notice, the tumble of events had prevented him from giving it more than random thought until tonight. The meeting was tomorrow morning, his wife had already said goodnight, and still the yellow pad was blank. Graves was troubled because he always did his homework, was scrupulously honest in his communications, and for the life of him couldn't figure out what to say.

Enrollment was holding up satisfactorily in the college as a whole as well as in the history survey courses. The general education requirements saw to that, and although periodic studies were undertaken, there was little sentiment for changing them. The problem was with the upper division courses. In this time of job consciousness among both faculty and students, the number of history majors had declined precipitously. There simply weren't enough students coming through to sustain the courses necessary for a history major. Thoughts of a liberal arts college without a history major sent a shudder up Graves's spine.

The history faculty was restless but not hostile. They viewed Graves as a friend and really wanted to hear what he had to say. Should he tell them that the future looks even bleaker than the present? Should he seek to inspire them to new arrangements and interdisciplinary ventures that had very little chance of success? Should he appeal to their sense of the flow of history itself and urge them to hold on and await the return of the swinging pendulum? Should he initiate a college-wide study committee and thus sidestep the issue for awhile? Although a rather bright man and widely experienced, Graves was seriously stuck on this one.

Even though the history faculty were quite friendly, Graves knew that he was being tested. The dean, after all, is an academic leader, and he was being called upon to lead. It simply wouldn't do to tell them that he, too, was stumped. Still the yellow pad was blank.

How would you advise Graves to proceed?

Response # 1

I suspect that Dean Graves has additional essential departments in which upper division enrollments are a special problem. Given the strength of the history survey courses, the total cost-effectiveness of the history department is likely to be favorable. If so, the tolerance level for small enrollments at the upper division level should increase.

History is one of many departments in a liberal arts college that need to be preserved as essential departments, and this decision includes the major courses as well as the lower division, general education courses. It is quite common to see departments with many students seeking additional faculty positions, while others are seeking to maintain their positions in the face of lower enrollments. As a general principle, the awarding of new positions should trail rather than satisfy enrollment demands. Similarly, the withdrawal of positions or programs should also trail enrollment declines.

Attempting to protect essential departments at the expense of the growth areas is an appropriate decision. Commitment to this kind of resource sharing is important to the overall esprit de corps of an institution. There is, however, a major problem accompanying this kind of strong commitment: Many departments lose their zeal for self-help when they believe their enrollment demands will not be met or when they believe that staffing and programs will be preserved regardless of enrollment declines.

In order to counteract this problem, departments such as history need to articulate for the dean the specific steps they are taking to improve their share of the available enrollments in lower as well as upper division courses. Are curriculum changes a partial answer? What about improvement in instructional methodology? Are the upper division courses attractive to nonmajors? Are there upper division courses that blend with major requirements in political science, sociology, art, communication, and other areas? Have such linkages been explored in an open and constructive manner? Is history doing all it can to help itself? A few of these questions might also be addressed to those departments with high enrollments.

Hopefully, the creativity of the faculty and the active leadership of the dean will help to preserve an essential department. I would certainly want to devote my first efforts to preservation. In fact, I suspect that I would even want to devote my last efforts to such a cause. (Otto F. Bauer, Vice Chancellor for Academic Affairs, University of Nebraska-Omaha.)

Response # 2

Deans need to recognize that departmental faculty in every discipline consider their teaching and research areas critical to the university and to the acquisition of a college education. Thus, it is important that the deans, in collaboration with the faculty and other administrators, develop contingency plans to be used in case of enrollment declines. These plans should be developed before the crisis appears. Because Graves does not have such a plan available, it would be helpful to delineate the strategies to be used when meeting with the history faculty. He might begin by listing the following background information on his yellow pad: (1) analysis of enrollment profile for history courses for the past five years; (2) development of a simple chart reflecting the enrollment pattern for distribution to the faculty; (3) comparison of enrollment data in other departments within the school.

It is important to be able to respond to questions that are likely to surface relative to enrollments. After making notes regarding the preceding data to be brought to the meeting, it is important that attention be given to the challenges Graves is to face.

Dean Graves needs to approach the faculty with basic enrollment facts in the major history courses covering a five-year span. This time period is necessary to avoid the argument that the data do not reflect the actual trend. Included with course enrollment data should be a chart depicting the student/faculty production of the history department as well as *that* of the humanities and social sciences departments. The productivity profile should give the faculty a sense of their status in comparison with faculty in other departments.

Graves must meet the faculty in a manner similar to the president of a major corporation who is faced with the possibility of losing the business unless immediate steps are taken through reductions and consolidation to salvage what had once been a productive business. In the case of the history department, the issue is one of supply and demand. Early in his remarks, Graves should make it known that the issue is not a philosophical discussion on the merits of history within the academy, but rather one of survival of a longstanding program. He will need to get the group to see that the problem is not a matter of arbitrarily eliminating a department, but rather of implementing essential survival strategies during this critical period.

The dean should begin by bringing to the attention of the faculty the data that he compiled, and in so doing share with them the unpleasant but realistic fact that the college/university cannot continue to support nonproductive programs. It is important for the dean to give his remarks with an air of concern, but positiveness. He might address the group in the following way.

Dean's Comments to the History Department

Colleagues, we are all aware that in recent years we have had a continuous drop in the number of students electing history as a major. It is indeed unfortunate that even though the history faculty comes in contact with practically every student at Seashore University, we have not been able to sell the notion to freshmen and sophomores that history is a viable major for students going into a number of professions and graduate schools. One wonders why we have not convinced our students that history could well be an appropriate undergraduate degree for careers in legal professions, government, museums, archives, communications and broadcasting, university teaching and administration, foreign service, and international corporate management.

Students may argue that one cannot enter these professions with an undergraduate degree. We as professionals need to point out to them that advanced study and a graduate degree are needed for most of the fields mentioned, regardless of the undergraduate degree.

What I am saying to you, colleagues, is that I am still convinced that history is a viable major for today's students. However, my opinion is of little worth unless you, the instructors in the history department, can sell your own discipline in a period when there are other majors with appeal to our students. As you well know, one can have a good product, but if the consumer is not buying it we have to find a way to package the product so that it appeals to the consumer. Otherwise, we are forced to use the other option—taking the product off the market. As I stand before you today, we face the same dilemma as the corporation when it comes to selling a major in history as a viable major to our undergraduate students.

In all candor, I must inform you that unless there is renewed interest in enrolling in advanced history courses, we will have to make personnel reductions. Where we will cut and whom we will displace remains uncertain at this time. I am suggesting, however, that we update our professional profile and identify any other areas of professional expertise that might be utilized at this university. Your updated professional profile should be forwarded to the Office of the Dean to be added to your personnel file. I would also suggest that if you have interest in pursuing a career change, you should bring that to our attention. The updated faculty profile should enable us to be more effective in assisting you in the likelihood that we would have to eliminate your position.

I recognize that personnel reduction is the least desirable option on your part as well as the administration's. Thus, I would like us to work together to find an alternative approach to our dilemma. As I agonized over our situation, I jotted down one or two approaches that we may take to increase enrollment in upper level courses.

We might review the requirements for a major in history to determine the possibilities of dropping some of the courses and restructuring other courses to include the content of those dropped. Let me hasten to say that I am not suggesting that we lower the quality of the program in history, but I am asking that you take a good hard look at redundancy. It might help to alleviate enrollment problems if we would not attempt to offer low-enrollment courses as often as we have in the past.

We may also address this problem through the advisement process. Students could be advised to take selected electives depending upon career goals. Such an approach gives them a broader foundation to pursue some of the career options mentioned earlier.

If we indeed feel it is critical that we preserve the department of history at this university, it means that we—the faculty in the department, recruitment officers, counselors, administrators, and the like—must take the initiative to let prospective students know of the viability of history to the educated person and as a foundation for a number of career options. Thus, I would like to appoint three persons from the department to an advisory team. This team would be charged with the responsibility of interacting with students, faculty within the department, alumni, counselors, and other persons the group deems necessary in order to provide the department as well as me with ideas for increasing the number of history majors. I would like to have your report within six weeks. Time is critical, for the establishment of the advisory team does not entirely alleviate the prospect of losing history as a major.

We must be cognizant of the fact that without an increased enrollment, it will be necessary to consider reduction of the department to a service area. This is a serious move and will not be considered without a feasibility study of the impact it would have on the total university. The decision on the establishment of a task force to consider the impact of the loss of history as a major will not be made until I have some indication of what you as a department will propose to the advisory team. I sincerely hope that we can rekindle the interest of our students in selecting history as a major field. You may be assured that I am available to work with you in a team relationship as we seek to revive and maintain this distinguished department. (Martha E. Dawson, Vice President for Academic Affairs, Hampton University, Hampton, Virginia.)

Both responses make it clear that extraordinary efforts may be necessary to preserve an essential department in the process of being abandoned by students. The first response (Vice Chancellor Bauer), in indicating that there are likely to be other departments in the same type of difficulty, causes one to wonder if a major shift in the mission of the institution may be approaching. If there is a serious mismatch between the interests of the clientele the institution is able to attract and the programs it has to offer, the institution may have to learn to attract a different clientele, change its mission, or prepare for further enrollment declines. The self-help suggestion in the first response is unfolded further in the second response (Vice President Dawson).

In recommending the establishment of an advisory team, Dawson seems to be placing the ball squarely in the department's court. If the dean can be persuaded that the department members have developed strategies to effectively deal with the situation, he may go with them for awhile at least. If the team fails or if its strategies fail, the second response indicates that the department may be preserved as a service area only, an outcome that the first respondent seems unwilling to take. In these matters there may be no good choices.

Experiential Education and Academic Standards

Most practices need to be reviewed periodically and traditions reevaluated to determine the degree to which they are still serving underlying values. Rarely, even in a traditional liberal arts context, is there only one way of doing things right. Academic standards can be invoked in defense of the merely familiar as well as the fundamentally essential, making it easier to oppose change for the wrong reasons. Deep within the professoriate is the cherished hope that students get value from taking courses. The suggestion that these values can be attained without a professorial intermediary flies in the face of the basic value structure of some academics, as the following case study shows.

CASE STUDY

As academic vice president, Jim Reeves wondered how he would be able to get his college ahead of events. Change had to occur, and that was so even in a liberal arts college profoundly committed to tradition. The cause of these reflections was the last general faculty meeting, when he had wondered out loud whether the college should revise its position against credit for prior experience. The Shakespeare authority, Christopher Marlowe, came right out of his seat at that point. His declamation was something to behold.

"Abandoning standards" was a constant refrain in his delivery. The gist of his message was that a liberal arts college had an obligation to be keepers of the gate. A liberal education should stand for something. It should include rigorous study and intimate acquaintance with certain classical traditions and figures.

At that point Molly Smith, a chemist, interrupted to ask where the students who were to be instructed in the delights of Shakespeare were going to come from. The freshman class, she pointed out, had been declining each fall from the previous spring for four years, and the demographic data for the northeast were certainly discouraging. That was the admissions office's responsibility, not his, Marlowe retorted. But even granted that conditions were getting tighter, Marlowe continued, surely relaxing standards was precisely the wrong response. He was even prepared to argue that what the college should do is tighten up, so that it "stood for something." Eventually, quality would be recognized and the college would once again flourish.

But would it? Jim Reeves didn't know. Under the circumstances, he did feel that the college ought to reflect the changed economic and social conditions of the times. Departments should be able to present their offerings in such a way that their importance was more self-evident to students. Recognizing the importance of the students' own prior accomplishment was one good way of doing this, Jim thought. This was especially so with regard to older students, an increasingly visible group over the past several years. Still, he knew that others besides Marlowe would contend that advocating such changes was just another way of subverting the importance of traditional approaches and values. It was caving in to the temper of the times, with its vocationalism, its emphasis upon quick payoffs for any work, and its indifference to established values and authority.

Others joined Molly in challenging Marlowe, but the meeting ended abruptly when the class bell rang. The cacophony of voices had indicated that there was no college consensus on the matter. Indeed, it was hard to sort out the issues, Jim reflected. He did wonder, for instance, how much of the resistance was to teaching a new type of student. Certainly the part-time and older students presented a new set of circumstances. Typically, they already had jobs and, perhaps more important, often seemed little disposed to stand in awe of the instructor. Indeed, they sometimes knew more than the faculty.

Whatever the factors, Jim did feel that he needed to do something. What would you recommend to him?

Response # 1

If the vice president surrenders the ground of high standards to faculty who advocate traditional forms of education, the battle is lost. Unless he moves quickly to change the form of the debate from a slogan swap to an informed discussion, the struggle will be over in a flash. He should use his connections and budget to inject new information into the dialogue: two or three articles on the assessment of experiential learning; a speaker from CAEL (Council for Adult and Experiential Learning); a sample portfolio from Empire State College or Alverno; an interview with an older student—to cite a few examples.

It is clear that Marlowe knows nothing of the good work done in this area in the last ten or fifteen years, and equally clear that logic and demographics will not unglue him from his position. The vice president, aided by other faculty, must now channel Marlowe's obvious concern for academic standards and the liberal arts tradition toward less traditional ways of honoring them.

Of course, it won't be easy. Some of Marlowe's vexation arises in the sadness he and others feel over the decline in the number and quality of younger students entering the college. His strong reaction to the vice president's ideas should not be viewed as a negative statement. It must be heard as an affirmation of a cherished value, as a signal of hope. But unless Marlowe is given more information on older students and on the assessment of prior learning, his intransigence may well block movement by the faculty. The challenge is to enlist Marlowe as a collaborator, to put his intelligence and forcefulness to better use. (John F. Noonan,

Dean, School of Arts and Sciences, Iona College, New Rochelle, New York.)

Response # 2

What should Jim Reeves do? First, identify the real changes he wants to see take place. Does he really want Christopher Marlowe to change his mind or does he want him to be quiet so that Molly Smith and company can work with the new types of students in peace? Does he want a change in the academic standards or two separate academic standards? Does he want some genuine conversation on academic standards and how they have changed in the past and how they might change in the future?

For the sake of argument I am going to assume that Jim Reeves is genuinely committed to getting his college "ahead of events." I would suggest that he plan a faculty forum on the issue of change, a second one on the history of change in academic standards at his own institution, and a third one in which the new students tell the faculty who they are and what they want from the college.

The first faculty forum on "The Great Change Makers" would have one outside speaker and five faculty speakers from different disciplines. One of these would be Professor Marlowe. The letter of invitation to Marlowe would indicate that since he taught Shakespeare, a dramatist who lived in a great age of change, surely he was an expert on the great change makers in the Renaissance. He would be asked to examine the kind of leadership that brings about change and the social conditions that made poetic change possible, and to define the nature of change in the English sixteenth century. Professor Marlowe is thus given an opportunity to "show his stuff," to show how the old can illuminate the new, and to speak with others instead of making declamations. Other faculty members who represent quite varied views would be chosen to speak. A moderator would be chosen who could genuinely manage what might be a wild and wooly occasion. Rules for the forum—on the Cambridge model—should be agreed upon so that no one can dominate and good thinking and wit can prevail. What this subject is going to need is wit in order for the anger to be contained and usefully engaged.

The second forum would be on the history of change in academic standards. This will take some research. I would focus the discussion on actual changes that have taken place in the last fifty years and do some archival research that would be full of interesting details and humor. Again, some questions need to be identified. For what students were these changes made? What was the curriculum like when the changes were made? Who was on the faculty when the changes were recommended? What was the world like at the time? Did any world event—the return of GIs from Korea, for example—change the curriculum or the standards of the college?

The third forum would be a kind of "Hearing the New Student's Voices." They would be asked three questions: Who are you? What do you want from your education? How does the institution need to change to meet your needs? Standards may not be the real issue for the students. Who knows what the real issues for these students are? The forum will enable the faculty to find out.

I would suggest to Jim Reeves that he ask faculty to commit themselves to attendence at all three forums. Whatever size this group turns out to be (say 30 out of 150 faculty), this is clearly a faculty group that will be charged to take the findings of the forums to the faculty at large. A consensus of some kind will emerge and Jim will have avoided one voice becoming the controller of that consensus. (Eva Hooker, Vice President for Academic Affairs, Saint John's University, Collegeville, Minnesota.)

Response # 3

Jim Reeves is about to discover that only two of the twelve million current students are "traditional," defined as being eighteen to twenty-two years olds, attending full time, and living on campus. A traditional liberal arts institution can evade demographic shifts, potentially indefinitely, but not in this case. The trend line for traditional admissions has been going down for four years. The institution's environment has changed.

Our first need is to define the problem, and Jim Reeves is part of it. His genteel concern is at least three years late. The occasion of a general faculty meeting is probably not the perfect forum for opening this issue on a positive note. With nothing constructive to propose, the floor is abandoned to voices loudly confused about the institution's changing needs. Reeves's hope that the departments will resolve the problem by repackaging their courses in more relevant form suggests that there is no college-wide process to plan the curriculum and also suggests that Reeves does not understand the problem himself. Everyone at the faculty meeting seems to agree that experiential education is in fact a matter of "relaxing standards."

Aside from the lack of leadership, we can not be surprised that the faculty would feel their integrity threatened when unknown programs are associated with known economic threats. Reeves's real challenge is to initiate some faculty and institutional development. Reeves has to have more accurate strategic planning than is available to him. This is not just a matter of demographic data, but rather the more complex process of helping the faculty to recognize the value and necessity of their participation in the planning and management of the whole institution. The traditional compartmentalization by which faculty concerns are limited to curriculum and faculty status issues is near the heart of the problem. Especially in a small liberal arts college, which lacks the resources for planning and institutional research that a larger institution takes for granted, the faculty must become involved with such areas as admissions. With luck and adequate participation, the planning process could define some clear goals for the college that would resolve whether or not a broader vision of the "student" is needed. Nontraditional students are not just a financial resource in times of recruitment peril, as Molly Smith argues; the faculty must become committed to bringing all students to their fullest potential. Even Shakespeare needed time to develop.

Aside from the problems of planning structure and leadership, Jim Reeves needs to give some attention to the confusion of rigorous study and curricular rigidity. Experiential education is simply not "vocationalism" or any other barbarian at the liberal arts gate. Liberal arts institutions must not confuse an intellectual tradition with a particular manner of teaching. Shakespeare will in time be as enthusiastically studied by way of compact discs and telecourses as he was by way of conventional lecturing. No educational template has a monopoly on rigor. Weekend colleges are going to develop; cooperative programs with industry are flourishing. The main cause of vocationalism appears to be less the narrowness of professional faculties than the unwillingness of liberal arts faculties to get involved. This "keeping of the gate" seems to preserve comfort more than standards.

Experiential education admittedly does bring change. Many

of the students seeking partial credit for their experience are older. They most frequently commute, while reserving time for their families and jobs. They naturally resent the blockade of admissions requirements (recent test scores), inflexible course scheduling, and office runaround we teach our freshmen to endure. On the other hand, the older students are also more mature. They are highly motivated and livelier in class than many undergraduates. They have frequently encountered job obsolescence or unsatisfying situations, and their aspirations have focus. Their grades are typically higher than average—traditional students can even feel threatened by the "unfair" competition. These are not students we want to exclude even when the traditional student numbers swell again.

Specifically, Jim Reeves needs to plan some faculty development. He has two main problems. The first is the hostility and confusion apparent at the faculty meeting. Christopher Marlowe must never have met an older student in class or in committee. Molly Smith already seems primed for some serious planning activity regarding the institution's development over the next few years. Reeves should first arrange some faculty development workshops, taking full advantage of the publications and activities of such groups as CAEL. Site visits to successful programs are highly productive. Reeves is going to have to be patient and flexible here; faculty education is a touchy subject to those who need it. He can expect conflict, and may even find it healthy for the faculty to engage in informed debate. No perfect plan for experiential education exists, and the faculty and administration will have to work for consensus.

Reeves's second problem is to ensure a quality experiential education program. He will first have to address a wide variety of institutional roadblocks to nontraditional students, beginning with the admissions process. There are a wide variety of tests to explore—CLEP, ACT, DANTES—in deciding how to grant credit. Faculty are usually unaware at this stage that experiential education programs grant credit for demonstrated knowledge and not for experience per se. If available tests are not appropriate, students normally develop a portfolio that requires faculty assessment, and this in turn requires the faculty to develop standards of evaluation. Some institutions grant credit for specific courses in their catalogues, while others permit a limited amount of "block credit" for the portfolio. With regard to Marlowe's concern, faculty directly control the standards of the program.

What Reeves and the faculty have not discovered is that experiential education is no threat to either quality or "standing for something." Experiential education programs grant limited course credit for knowledge and skills the students bring to college, which is no more threatening than advanced placement credit. An office manager may prove that he or she has mastered freshman composition. It is conceivable that a professional Shakespearian actor might test out of Professor Marlowe's own rigorous tragic survey, freeing time for a more advanced course. Giving a thirty-five-year-old mother credit for a handful of general education requirements is simply not going to swamp classical traditions in a mire of "quick payoffs" and indifference to authority.

It is tough to accommodate change, and Reeves has a job before him. With persistent information, though, the attitudes that define an institution will change before the nontraditional students find another institution's nontraditional program more satisfactory. (Donald C. Stuart, Vice President for Academic Affairs, Longwood College, Farmville, Virginia.)

All three responses recognize that the root of the problem lies in faculty ignorance about experiential education. The first response (Dean Noonan) proposes that an informed discussion is needed and that Professor Marlowe should be enlisted as a collaborator in its development. The second response (Vice President Hooker) suggests accomplishing this by way of a faculty forum series in which Marlowe is a speaker. The third response (Vice President Stuart) sees the administration, and Jim Reeves in particular, as part of the problem. In addition to informational campaigns, Vice President Stuart proposes to forge a link between the problem and institutional planning and development. Through this planning and development, he believes, a faculty-accepted quality experiential education program is more likely. All three responses have resolved the dilemma by seeing it as an opportunity rather than a problem.

A time-honored administrative strategy is to enlist the opposition. Identifying ways to secure Marlowe's energies and attention in familiar and comfortable ways is a good first step toward changing his mind on the unfamiliar and uncomfortable issues to which he objects. When opposition occurs, deans and provosts should examine it carefully. On occasion, this examination will yield clues permitting the resolution of otherwise intractable problems.

Crossing Disciplinary Boundaries

The continuing attention of most academics is riveted tightly to their departments. When they look afield, it is usually toward their own discipline in another institution. When interdisciplinary activities are considered, it is usually in regard to research. Curricular activities that span several departments or are suspended between them invoke minimal ownership. For these reasons such activities, even when started with enthusiasm, sink lower and lower in the priority structure when the initiator moves on or when the circumstances change.

Interdisciplinary activities are difficult to start in a financial zero-sum situation. Too many people realize that funds diverted for their support must come from somewhere and everyone is busy guarding his or her departmental boundaries. New activities can often be undertaken only by letting go of older, less successful activities. There is little enthusiasm in academe for releasing older activities. A considerable amount of political savvy and academic skill is required to initiate and sustain interdisciplinary courses and programs. This savvy and skill must usually come from deans and provosts.

CASE STUDY

Dean Brewer was really enthused about the prospects of the meetings that had been set up between his art and music departments and the colleges of business and engineering. The music department was proposing an interdisciplinary program with business aimed at educating and training students for the music business in Nashville, and art was talking with engineering about an interdisciplinary graphics design major. Since Brewer had long been an advocate of interdisciplinary efforts, he was pleased to see that his faculty was finally responding.

He was further elated when the provost's office called to arrange a meeting of the fine arts, business, and engineering deans to discuss some practical matters that would help facilitate these efforts if they persisted and came to fruition.

The meeting started off quite well, with all parties speaking to their interest in these ventures. The provost was particularly eloquent in urging them onward. The initial "practical matters" were manageable, the deans thought. Changes in expectations for promotion and tenure and redefinition of research and public service would be contested by the faculty senate, of course, but the deans were convinced that, proceeding gradually and given time, they could work their decanal magic on the campus political machinery to clear such hurdles. The provost delighted them with the news that the president had agreed to his surprise recommendation that several scholarships be set aside to support students in these emergent programs. So far, so good.

The wet blanket came in the provost's announcement that although he was willing to bend the rules about what kinds of expenses could be charged to which accounts, there would be no new money to support these programs. He explained again his and the president's view that funds should be deployed maximally to the colleges, with only emergency reserves held centrally. They would have to get together and figure out how to fund the programs. The provost assured them that he would be quite likely to support whatever plan the three of them agreed to. They set another date for a progress report meeting a month hence, and went their own way.

Brewer knew that he and the other deans had followed through on the president's and provost's strategy of putting the money to work rather than holding sizable reserves. In fact, from Brewer's point of view, the money was all locked into worthwhile efforts in his college, and he readily saw that the same was true for the other deans. Brewer knew that the faculty took a long time agreeing in principle to these ventures. They had, after all, proposed them. He also knew that they were quite aware and concerned about the zero-sum game implications of what they were proposing. He wondered how far they would be willing to go when redeployment of resources had to be faced.

There were some prospects for external funding. Brewer estimated that even in the best of worlds, they might go a third of the way in providing what was needed. The other two-thirds would have to be provided from funds already allocated to the three colleges.

Brewer was aware that the provost had tossed them the ball. The three deans seemed resolute in trying to find ways to help these ventures succeed. They clearly had a planning problem, and those were the kind that Brewer liked best.

What options and alternatives should Brewer be thinking about?

Response # 1

Dean Brewer is an astute academic politician. He knows that his fine arts college desperately needs an influx of enrollments, while both the engineering and business colleges are trying to find ways to put a curb upon rapidly growing student numbers. He needs these new "career-oriented" fine arts programs much more than do the other deans. He also understands clearly that change—any change—is viewed with a great deal of skepticism within academia. Interdisciplinary programs, however well conceived and noble of purpose, are especially vulnerable during campus budget hearings. Because no one has any sense of ownership of them, interdiciplinary programs inevitably receive the lowest priority. Dean Brewer's objective has to be to give his fellow deans a sense of ownership, and in so doing subtly demonstrate the benefits for their business and engineering enterprises.

At this typical university, the provost allocates resources primarily according to student enrollment figures. Dean Brewer needs to develop his strategy upon this essential fact. He estimates that the two new programs will generate approximately twenty-five majors each within two years. His negotiations with the two other deans might contain the following elements:

1. The college of fine arts faculty would assume all of the time-consuming advising responsibilities. It would also assume responsibility for advertising the program to prospective students.

2. The curriculum for the programs will primarily utilize existing courses in business and engineering so no new major allocation of faculty resources would be required.

3. The curriculum would contain only two or three new capstone courses, which would seek to integrate the fine arts com-

poncnt with the business/engineering, component. Dean Brewer would give his fellow deans the option of whether his or their faculty would teach the courses. If additional training is required to prepare faculty for these new courses, he should provide the funding from his faculty development budget.

Dean Brewer's strategy should be tied to long-term and not short-term goals. Within a few years, his enrollments will be increased significantly and he will be able to talk to students about promising careers within the areas of music and art. The strategy designed here is nonthreatening to the other deans and essentially removes any inherent reasons for their not wishing to participate. They cannot even use the convenient and oft-employed tactic of accreditation constraints. By proposing a curriculum based primarily upon existing faculty resources and existing courses, and by being flexible in the development of the capstone courses, Dean Brewer should have his fellow deans in the bag. (Richard O. Davies, Vice President for Academic Affairs, University of Nevada-Reno.)

Response # 2

Dean Brewer confronts a familiar predicament in the lean years of higher education in the 1980s: a sound new curricular idea, one that even has widespread support, for which little institutional new money is available. Dean Brewer has the responsibility of encouraging curricular reform at a time when, without additional funding, many faculty members' initial reaction will be to simply continue business as usual. The options the dean needs to consider are ones that minimize this latter, unhappy outcome.

The situation intially may look bleak, but there are a surprisingly large number of positive signs surrounding the proposal. First, it has strong administrative support; not only are all three deans committed to making it work—not a negligible accomplishment since the "hot" areas of engineering and business often tend to go their own ways—but also the central administration is clearly behind the projects. The provost took the initiative to bring the deans together to discuss implementation, and he seems willing vocally to support the projects. Further, although no new money is available, the president signaled his support through allocation of scholarships for these new programs. Finally, the prospects for some external funding, albeit at a modest level, may well be propitious. It would provide necessary seed money to strengthen support within the faculty for these new interdisciplinary endeavors.

Of course, the lack of new institutional money puts a damper on enthusiasm for these projects, and without it there is the ever present threat of faculty resistance. Dean Brewer is aware that the faculty agreed to these new ventures only in principle, but also that the faculty had proposed the programs and knew of the possibility of having to fund them internally. The challenge that Dean Brewer faces is determining how far he can go in pushing implementation without generating faculty backlash.

To maximize the possibility of bringing this proposal to fruition, Dean Brewer should adopt certain general strategies. First, the programs represent a wonderful opportunity for faculty development. Not only will faculty within the disciplines be able to learn new things; they will begin conversations across disciplinary boundaries. This opportunity, coupled with appeals to faculty who would enjoy this kind of activity, should be a key element in Dean Brewer's strategies.

Second, the dean should go after external funding that might be available. It can make a significant impact and be used to entice more faculty support for the projects. The dean needs to make it clear that some of this money will be spent for faculty growth opportunities.

Third, the availability of scholarship monies, provided with the president's blessing, should not go unnoticed on Dean Brewer's campus. This financial support from the top is a strong inducement that needs publicizing. New scholarship opportunities interest faculty and departments as ways to recruit good, new students. New students are significant to faculty, especially in areas of declining or potentially declining enrollments. Dean Brewer and his faculty should recognize this in art and music.

In developing a specific action plan, a most important step to enhance the likelihood of success is to open up information about the current situation at all levels of the community. The deans should meet again, review the results, and discuss the mutual advantages they see in these programs. Dean Brewer should sit with his department chairs in music and art, explain where things stand, and reinforce the important roles these programs can play in maintaining enrollments, in providing larger opportunities for students, and in humanizing the business and technical worlds.

In addition, the deans and department chairs should meet with faculty who agreed in principle to the plans in order to elicit their continued cooperation. Finally, Dean Brewer should not ignore the potential impact that students interested in such programs can have on faculty thinking. To the extent to which there is student interest and concern on campus about such career opportunities within the arts, Dean Brewer should discuss with these students the avenues that these programs make available and encourage their support.

Once these various constituencies are informed and involved, Dean Brewer has a good chance to begin some kind of implementation structure. If external funding becomes available, it can be used for faculty workshops and seminars to begin the conversion process so important to the success of such programs. In addition, Dean Brewer can elicit support from faculty for pilot ventures in these areas, utilizing, first, some existing curricular structures that can be shaped to this new purpose. In the end, if these pilot projects yield positive results, Dean Brewer and his colleagues will be in a stronger position to achieve the more significant changes that institutionalize these new programs within the academic life of the university. (G. Benjamin Oliver, Dean of Arts and Sciences, Southwestern University, Georgetown, Texas.)

Response # 3

Dean Brewer has encountered the perfect "good news, bad news" scenario. He also has been taught marvelous lessons in "hindsight/foresight." All issues in higher education administration will inevitably return to a discussion concerning budget. Funds allocated, in the minds of most faculty, are equated with institutional support. Although a lesson has been taught, and undoubtedly learned, Dean Brewer must still deal with the situation as it is, and resolve the dilemma as best he can.

The first step in dealing with any administrative problem is the identification of the elements. Each of the costs associated with the new programs must be accurately listed: faculty salaries (current as well as new), supplies, library materials, new equipment, and support staff. Without listing these costs exactly, none of the deans will be able to find a common middle ground.

The second step will be to identify the areas of overlap. What faculty will be retained in the new program? What new faculty will be needed? What support staff are truly necessary for the function of the new program? Are substantial amounts of library materials and supplies necessary, and at the same time what requirements may be released in other areas through a concentration on this new program? Supplies and materials revolve around faculty members themselves. If faculty members are reassigned, the associated costs must be reassigned with them. Simultaneously, the deans should identify the areas of the new costs, to delineate areas of overlap with existing programs.

With regard to the old and overlapping budgets, as well as to the new ones, the deans should evaluate each expenditure area for potential grant support. Outside funding can be used not only to encourage new ventures, but also to reward what an institution is already doing well and wishes to do better.

At this point, the deans may see that the true amount for the new program is already considerably reduced. Then they will identify areas of specific budgetary possibilities for each of the components remaining uncovered: financial aid, library, capital funds, etc. If other offices are involved with these expenditures—i.e., financial aid or library—tactful negotiations with each of them may produce a reasonable reallocation.

Once the three deans have done all their homework, they should then be able to return to the provost—united—showing what has already been done. At this point they can ask for the remaining amount from emergency reserves, but with several potential compromises already in mind: (1) an incremental approach to funding over a series of months or even years; and (2) a willingness to defer certain expenditures until the end of the fiscal year, when the provost could roll over the cost to the succeeding fiscal year or use left-over monies from the expiring year.

The deans will have then shown the faculty that they have made every effort to address the question of budget. Given the quality of the relationships between the faculty and the deans, two results are possible: (1) The faculty, though they will probably complain, will have faith that their needs may eventually be covered and proceed with the new program; or (2) the faculty will reevaluate the need for the new programs and will determine that what they are currently doing is worth more to them than the sacrifice necessary to initiate the new programs. All of the deans' reasonable efforts—showing enrollment projections, benefits to the departments' growth potential, and the effect on retention of faculty—will play an important role in this final step.

No problem of this complexity has a simple answer; however, the deans must anticipate at the very beginning the raising of the issue of budget. The resolution of this issue, or at least some strategies to address it, must be in any provost's or dean's mind before embarking on such negotiations with faculty. (Gregg Lacy, Dean of Academic Affairs, Keuka College, Keuka Park, N.Y.).

Each of the three responses proposes a different strategic framework. The first response (Vice President Davies) focuses attention on negotiations between the deans. The second (Dean Oliver) concentrates on convincing the faculty that the interdisciplinary programs are in their long-term interest. The third (Dean Lacy) provides a step-by-step analysis of how to meet both of these problems. All three reponses converge on the realization that the real problem is the budget.

In any interdisciplinary effort, attention must be paid to the impact of individual faculty participation upon tenure and promotion considerations. Similarly, careful attention must be paid to the distribution and recording of student credit hours generated. The institutional academic accounting system plays an important role in faculty response to interdisciplinary programming.

Although none of the respondents specifically points it out, it may be implicit in their responses that if one or more of the deans gives up, any hope of these interdisciplinary efforts reaching fruition is lost. The deans have an intellectual leadership opportunity and responsibility in these matters. Provosts may be well advised to test the deans' resolve before committing substantial institutional resources. If these programs succeed, it will be because the deans, with their faculties, made them succeed. Such is the call of intellectual leadership.

Problems With the PE Major

The entanglement of academics with intercollegiate athletics has long been a decidedly mixed blessing for many institutions. A few have been able to keep academics and athletics in mutually supportive roles, but more have found success to be elusive. Not infrequently, faculty will rally to the academic banner, and alumni and some trustees to the external importance of athletics, leaving the administration caught in between. An adept dean of health, physical education and recreation is often the focal point for obtaining a workable balance. The following case study illustrates some of the difficulties involved.

CASE STUDY

While the university was hardly known as a jock's school, it did have a longstanding positive reputation for preparing secondary PE majors for the state's high schools. Dean Griffiths was known and respected throughout the state for his role in turning out a good product. He had balanced academic ability with athletic prowess and built the college of HPER to the point where it had been able to become considerably more selective in its admissions.

All that started to shift three years ago with the trustees' decision to upgrade athletics and go for Division I NCAA status. The coaches were vigorously recruiting star athletes from a five-state area, many of whom were extremely poor academic risks, and almost all of whom wanted to major in PE. Several had been admitted to the university, but could not qualify for admission to HPER. Dean Griffiths knew that some would never play for the university because they would be on academic probation after one semester.

Griffiths approached the AD and coaches for a sizable increase in tutoring funds, but was unsuccessful. The coaches said the students were his responsibility academically and he should not expect a solution by taxing athletics. The rest of the university hasn't thought too kindly of remedial work in general and was unlikely to provide funding.

Griffiths knew he had to hold the line on academic standards. He had staunch support from the academic vice president in that regard. Yet, to flunk out too many athletes would clearly stir up a major brouhaha.

What options and alternatives does Dean Griffiths have and how would you advise him?

Response # 1

The first thing Dean Griffiths must do is fully and honestly examine his convictions on the matter, and decide what personal and professional price he is willing to pay to sustain those convictions. He must do this understanding that there is no feasible alternative to the decision to move to Division I status, and therefore no likelihood that many of the athletes admitted within that decision will be able to achieve and maintain the academic standards he has worked to establish in the school of health, physical education and recreation. This is a showdown situation, and the dean has to face it for what it is.

If, in that context, he continues to *know* that he has to hold the line on academic standards, he must make that position firmly clear to the academic vice president, who is presumed to be in staunch support, but whose staunchness might weaken a bit if it were clear that such support would bring him as well into a probable confrontation with the board of trustees. Dean Giffiths also must have a clear and accurate idea of where his faculty stand, for without their full support there is no way he can maintain a position. The vice president must inform his president exactly what the stakes are in the situation, and report the president's likely position to the dean.

There are two major parts to the dean's concern, which may or may not be separable in his mind. One relates to admission to the school. Reference to tutoring funds already in use suggests that admissions standards, the dean's fond belief notwithstanding, are already at a fairly low level. He might reasonably conclude, provided his admissions committee is solidly behind him, that a few more politic exceptions to a desired standard might not much alter things.

Once admitted, there is the second problem of retention and eligibility. This is within the dean's influence, but not within his control, unless the faculty are a lot more docile than the school's academic reputation suggests. If the athletes cannot find enough sympathetic faculty, the certainty then is that a fair number will be quickly in eligibility trouble. At that point the dean can do three things, singly or in combination. He can, in effect, say, "I told you so" and stonewall the complainers; he can, not unreasonably, argue that it is his faculty, not him, who are insisting on the troublesome academic standards, and take such refuge as is possible in arguments of shared responsibility and academic freedom; or he can, with this added leverage in an urgent situation, go back to the coaches, who might now be a bit more amenable, for more tutoring funds. The first choice, by itself, is likely to leave him principled but unemployed, or at least reassigned. The others promise no good solution, but perhaps might buy some time for the situation to work itself out in some so-far-unseen ways.

The dean's options and alternatives in this situation are, in short, few and all distasteful. If he wants to keep his job for any period of time, he will have to make some important compromises. Nothing in the history of athletic escalation in this country gives any ground to the hope that the board, having made this decision, will accept any argument to reverse it or to temper its consequences. The trouble with compromises is that little ones often force bigger ones, so that what one buys from them is not a solution but a bit of time to make clear that a good solution really is not possible. If the dean really believes what he is said to stand for in this case, the only practical advice to him is to start looking for a job at an institution more compatible with his values. (George R. Healy, retired, former Provost, College of William and Mary, Williamsburg, Virginia.)

Responses # 2

It is not a good idea to stand on principle very often. Deans who do so are usually pure and righteous—and also regularly unemployed. Rigid adherence to immovable principles does not allow for negotiation, compromise, change, and reasonable discourse. Yet, there are a few rare occasions when one has to dig in and fight. Dean Griffiths may be facing one.

Athletic programs need not warp or ruin academic programs, and it would be unwise of Dean Griffiths to be so pristine as to reject the new (and less able) athletic recruits out of hand. But the situation with which he is presented has the earmarks of an inappropriate "professional" sports program. The tip-off is the refusal of the athletic director to fund an academic support program for intellectually weak or unprepared athletic recruits. When those responsible for a sports program conclude that the education of athletes is a low priority (or no priority at all), a serious crisis exists.

No doubt a "fire storm" will develop, but perhaps this is what Dean Griffiths' university needs. And if he doesn't blow the whistle on the play, who will?

If Dean Griffiths decides to stand and fight, he would be well-advised to consider carefully what he is fighting about. It is easy, in such situations, to begin believing that one's own program goals are the only ones appropriate to the university. For example, if the athletic director were persuaded to modify his program—to avoid athletic recruits who are manifestly unqualified to deal with the university's academic program (regardless of their athletic abilities) and to provide academic support for borderline cases— then Dean Griffiths ought to be ready to compromise, perhaps by developing a "second track" within the HPER major. In other words, one wants to be sure one is really standing on principle, not on a program concept or a personal commitment to a particular way of doing things.

Dean Griffiths may also want to think about seeking employment elsewhere. The board of trustees is responsible for the university's policies, including its policies on athletics. If these policies are (or become) truly contrary to Dean Griffiths's fundamental and professional principles, he may want to make an issue of it, but he must recognize that his professional life at this university is likely to end soon. Perhaps it should. A board that is prepared to sacrifice a strong academic program to intercollegiate athletics does not deserve the service of a good dean. (Charles S. Olton, Vice President for Academic Affairs and Dean of the Faculty, Barnard College, Columbia University, New York.)

Response # 3

Dean Griffiths's problem is more than the usual battle of standards between secondary PE majors and jocks. Athletic programs can take off on their own, driven by the collective interests of star athletes, coaches, boosters, and hyperactive alums. No other program normally has such independence on campus, but with television alone providing more than $1 million a year to Division I productions, we have more than enough motives and means for trouble. Despite recent extensive media attention and some dramatic court cases, one suspects that neither the NCAA nor the more academic intercollegiate associations are going to provide Dean Griffiths with any quick solution to his worries. Nor will the minimal standards generated by Proposition 48 and the "no pass–no play" policies of a growing number of high schools eliminate the dean's problem.

Since Dean Griffiths has vice-presidential backing for tough academic standards, one is tempted to advise him to welcome the fire storm he fears. He can preach loftily of excellence and send the miscreants off to academic probation and suspension by simply flunking them. This will either drive the athletes to other majors or force the athletic staff to reconsider their approach to academics. This option is simple; the other options will mire the dean in the enormously more complex process of educating a number of underprepared students and athletic staff.

Since Dean Griffiths wants to maintain a respectable program, he can not avoid the administrative politics of reallocating resources. His first task is to identify and begin to work on the various constituencies who are committed to Division I success. Through the academic vice president, he has to send a message to the president and trustees that their decision to upgrade athletics absolutely requires more than a stadium, uniforms, and recruitment money. Their priorities determine the direction of the institution, and the same policy must be clear to both the academic administration and the athletic program. If the top administration is weak or divided on developing an adequate policy on the recruitment and admission of weak students, Dean Griffiths will have to return to the fire storm.

Most presidents and trustees are, however, committed to educational success, even for athletes. Dean Griffiths needs to turn to the immediate source of his problem—the athletic director and the coaches. They may think that academic success is not their problem, but a strong case can be made that it is. Assuming that they ignore the broader ideals of sports programs involving sound bodies and minds, they still have a major problem on their hands as their athletes become ineligible or are returned home. It is not Dean Griffiths's problem alone; the students will shift to other majors if the PE requirements prove impossible.

The athletic director is the key figure here. He or she has to develop the same retention programs that other institutions have found to be necessary. The football and basketball coaches will probably be the first to complain, but they are used to being used as cash cows in the athletic program, and they have the most to gain if their recruits are academically solid. If the institution is going to have tough standards, and is unwilling to allocate special retention resources for the star athletes, the athletic program must develop its own tutorial and remediation service. The athletic director can find a variety of successful retention programs to use as models.

The last important constituency is the alums and boosters, and their interest in tutoring can be expected to be minimal. But they do want successful teams, and this will require athletes in good standing. They will not block a good retention program.

Dean Griffiths's best option, thus, is to convince the administration and the athletic staff that academic quality must be preserved and that good retention programs are available and affordable for the athletic program. He has to approach the athletic director more forcefully. Events and bad press may force the NCAA to take stronger positions on academic standards and progression, but Dean Griffiths had better take the initiative with his problem. One might almost yearn for the old days before freshman-eligibility rules developed. (Donald C. Stuart, Vice President for Academic Affairs, Longwood College, Farmville, Virginia.)

Each of the responses provides practical advice for dealing with this problem. The first response (Vice President Healy) suggests that the dean should really think through all that is involved in this situation, including whether he should look for another position. The compromises that are seen as necessary to resolve the problem may not be compromises the dean is willing to make. The second response (Vice President Olton) provides a similar view and targets the athletic director as the key individual, along with the dean, in making the compromises work. The third response (Vice President Stuart) concentrates on the administrative politics of dealing with the president, vice president for academic affairs, and trustees on the one hand and the athletic director and coaches on the other in developing an adequate retention program. This is the long way around, and in the end might not work. Some situations with which deans and provosts work do not have happy endings. This might be one of them. If so, the workable choices, should the dean decide that it's worth it to stay on and try harder, are likely to take the form of damage control. While there are times when damage control is essential, there are no times when it's pleasant work.

College Prerogatives in Accepting Outsiders

Shifts of faculty within and among colleges, schools, and departments are no longer uncommon as institutions respond to changing student and societal interests and to budgetary problems and disciplinary developments. Some shifts are facilitated by elaborate retraining programs. Others are not. In either case, questions of tenure and hospitality are important. The following case deals with the displacement of faculty from underenrolled departments and their reception in another academic department.

CASE STUDY

Doug Cooper felt quite uncomfortable when pondering how to respond to the new provost. The provost's proposition that he, and hence the college of education, make room for faculty being transferred from history and foreign languages was very troublesome. The experience of five years ago was still in his mind— when the former provost had "requested" that the college of education make a place for the university vice president for external relations, who was stepping down after many years of service. Too young to retire and too distant from his original academic discipline for that department to accept him, this person had neither taught not pursued a research project for over a decade. Yet, the provost felt an obligation to him and had identified the college of education as the logical spot for him. Even though the university had provided the college a special budget supplement covering his extra salary, the faculty members of the college had not welcomed this development. It had too much of a special-deal flavor to it and violated their sense of college autonomy and prerogatives. As a result, the individual had never really been completely integrated into college activities.

The present situation, Cooper feared, would have the same result. It was too bad that the history department had more faculty than it could support, and everyone felt sorry for the fortunes of the foreign language department. But it was ridiculous to expect the college of education to absorb two extra faculty just because one had a master's degree in the history of education and the other one a similar degree in language education. Granted that the university was the environment and context for all of the colleges, it was still important to recognize that each college had its own integrity and prerogatives. Surely, Dean Cooper's faculty would believe that it was appropriate for him to strenuously resist the provost's recent attempt to palm off these two on the college of education. The faculty just wouldn't allow itself to be seen as a dumping ground without a considerable struggle.

They were genuine faculty, of course, rather than administrators, but it was still the case that the initiative was coming from without. The dean of arts and sciences as well as the history and foreign language chairs had earlier approached Cooper to discuss the possibility of their transfer as the budget situations in their departments had become tighter. Cooper had been quite cool to the idea and had sought to discourage any further discussion. Now, though, it was clear that they had gotten the provost's ear.

He wondered whether they were retaliating for his failure to support the movement to increase the number of required general education courses. Both the history and foreign language departments would have benefited by that curricular change. It would not have worked to the advantage of the college of education, though, as it already had too many requirements mandated by the state department of education. Consequently, Cooper had lobbied against the general education proposal.

Cooper wished that he were on surer ground with the provost. In his first year at the institution, the provost had come with a reputation as a hot-shot organizational theorist. In fact, he had published what was still regarded as the leading text on the new humanism in management. From all that Cooper could see, however, the provost was one of those whose behavior was at odds with his speech. For while the provost was always happy to speak at length about the events of participatory management, his own behavior seemed quite hierarchical and authority-laden. He seemed reluctant to share information or provide feedback and did little delegating. As a result, Cooper was uncertain how to approach him or what strategy to take when he did.

Cooper would have to act soon, though, and he needed to start with his own faculty. He had taken enough flack from them over the former vice president that he did not want once again to appear to be mere putty in the hands of the administration. He knew he ran that risk in bringing the issue up with them. On the other hand, was it wise to take on the provost without having first talked to the faculty?

What strategy should Cooper adopt?

Response # 1

Decades of growth within higher education have produced a generation of older college administrators without the experience to deal with the circumstances of stable enrollments or of decline and retrenchment. Neither is there a sizable body of literature or a heritage of academic tradition to guide the hands of younger administrators who must deal with new conditions.

Within memory, growth and change have been constant bedfellows. Enrollments doubled, tripled, and took quantum leaps as major institutions emerged from the small colleges of yesterday. Changes that resulted meant that one should never become comfortable in one's office because it would probably be located somewhere else tomorrow. Mistakes in hiring did not really matter because new, more competent people could always be hired. Individuals who became ineffective could be reassigned because new positions could be created. Few negative tenure decisions had to be made because the increase in the size of departments would take care of the critical matters of diversity and flexibility. Focus was always on the new, the additional. It seemed as if expansion were the major characteristic of the university.

But, the Golden Age is behind us. Growth has slowed dramatically and, in many situations, enrollment stability is the best to be hoped for. In many cases, decline has been in evidence for a number of years.

The slowdown and the decline have necessitated new ways of dealing with change. Change must not be resisted. It is desirable, even necessary. In fact, one of the things to be feared most is that stasis will set in and academic dryrot and atrophy will result. When the needs of society change, and student interests shift, the university needs to flex and change and shift in response.

As the enrollment stabilizes across the institution, or even declines, enrollments within departments and schools continue to shift. These shifts must not be stopped or the institution will lose its vitality and will cease meeting societal needs. The only restraints should be those that would control the rate of growth and decline in academic units. The total institution must maintain a certain balance, and no department or school should be permitted such monolithic growth that the overall balance of the institution is distorted.

Departments that continue to grow need additional faculty; departments that lose enrollments do not need all the faculty they have. If one were dealing with widgets instead of human beings, the solution would be obvious—hire new faculty and staff where they are needed, and release those where they are no longer needed. Such a solution, however, rapidly becomes a nonsolution. There is no surer way to tear apart an institution. It will become like an armed camp. Departments will be lined up against departments and students will join the fray. Such a situation must be avoided if at all possible.

The only way to hold the institution together and avoid this kind of bloodbath is to give assurances that no tenured faculty or staff will be let go if the rate of enrollment shifting can be controlled. One must be willing to live with the situation of many totally tenured departments after the untenured are not reappointed. Retraining and retooling incentives for tenured faculty must be provided in order to ensure continued vitality and dynamism. While faculty would still be housed in their respective departments in order to protect seniority rights, up to half of their teaching assignments may be made in other departments. In some cases where both sending and receiving departments are amenable, complete shifts of a faculty line may be made.

None of these situations will be popular. There will be grumbling and complaining, but they will be seen as the lesser of the evils. It is the old story of hanging together or most assuredly hanging separately. A majority of faculty will grudgingly settle for tentative no layoff and detenuring guarantees.

Where unionism exists, the provost and Dean Cooper could not make such a deal. All agreements would have to be worked out with the bargaining agent. Even if the faculty in this case were not unionized, Dean Cooper would be well advised to act as if it were. He needs to have serious discussions with his faculty and the provost. Agreements should be reached and tradeoffs secured. He should not bypass his faculty and make any deals with the provost; likewise, he should not stand up and say no to the provost. He should play the larger role of negotiator and mediator toward the goal of keeping the institution intact, with the realization that the greater institutional good is also in the best interests of each member of the institution. (Gordon I. Goewey, retired, formerly Vice President for Academic Affairs and Provost, Trenton State College, Trenton, New Jersey.)

Response # 2

An analysis of the situation that Dean Cooper is currently in reveals the following options:

1. It is possible that the faculty would actually accept the two faculty members whom the provost is palming off on the college of education. If so, it would be unwise for Cooper to oppose the transfer of the two faculty.
2. The provost may already be committed to the transfer and there may be nothing Cooper can do to prevent it. Opposing the transfer may do nothing more for Cooper than to cause a problem between him and the provost.
3. The faculty in the college of education may be adamantly opposed to the transfer of the two individuals and may truly expect Cooper to oppose the transfer at all costs.
4. The provost may be simply probing Dean Cooper to determine the level of resistance against the transfer. The provost may withdraw his proposal quickly if he sees it is firmly opposed by the dean and the faculty in the college.

I suggest that prior to talking with the faculty, Cooper have an informal conversation with the provost and attempt to find out how committed he is to the idea. Cooper should make the provost aware of his concerns about the transfer, emphasizing that the faculty in the college will view the provost as acting in an arbitrary and capricious fashion if he follows through with a transfer that is opposed by the faculty. I do not believe it is necessary at this stage for Cooper to talk to the faculty in his college as it appears that he knows quite well what their reaction will be.

If, after talking with the provost, he discovers that the provost is not unalterably committed to the transfer, but would really like the transfer to occur, Cooper should exploit this situation by attempting to secure from the provost some significant concessions in return for support of the transfer. If the provost is willing to make concessions, then Dean Cooper should favor the transfer and attempt to sell it to the faculty in the college.

The major step for Cooper is to ascertain the exact position of the provost. This should be done in a personal conversation and not through the exchange of memoranda. After ascertaining the provost's stance on this, Cooper should ask for concessions if the provost is committed to the transfer. If no concessions are forthcoming, then, Cooper will have to oppose the transfer and attempt to force the provost to change his mind. (He should begin reading the last section of the *Chronicle of Higher Education* closely at this stage.) Cooper needs to convince the provost of the necessity for there to be a quid pro quo solution to this situation. Neither the provost nor the dean wins with unpopular forced transfers.

This case study presents a specific example of an all-too-typical problem of higher education administration—the situation where an administrator finds himself in a dilemma in deciding whose side to take in a conflict. Does he support the faculty on this issue against the provost or does he support the provost in going against the wishes of the faculty? If the situation comes down to such extreme choices, it is very difficult for the dean to succeed. Obviously, he cannot function if he loses the respect of the faculty or if he is in constant conflict with the provost. The most important suggestion I could make in this situation is for the dean to make a special effort to be in very close communication and cooperation with the provost.

As the provost is new and probably does not know the faculty as well as the dean does, the dean has a responsibility to present accurately the opinions of his faculty to the provost and to describe what the reactions of the faculty will be in such a situation. The dean, in order to function well, needs to move the conflict away from either of the extremes presented. The first step is to establish a very close relationship with the provost. If he finds this is not possible, he then needs to look at other employment alternatives. (Donald E. Bowen, Vice President for Academic Affairs, Southwest Missouri State University, Springfield, Missouri.)

Both respondents recognize the importance of the role of the dean as negotiator and mediator between the faculty and the provost. In fact, the college dean's divided attention and loyalties parallel the department chairperson's. In each case, the faculty and upper-level administration looks to the dean and chair to advocate their positions. The first response (former Vice President Goewey) speaks of tradeoffs. The second response (Vice President Bowen) speaks of a quid pro quo, but advises that it may be desirable for the dean to seek other employment if the negotiations fail. More and more often, a situation is polarized to the point where someone's job is on the line. In these situations, we may not need tougher administrators. We may need smarter ones.

CHAPTER FOUR

Redirecting Difficult People

AFTER A FEW YEARS in office, many deans and provosts come to realize that most administrative problems are at heart "people" problems. Even those that appear to be primarily budget problems readily translate into personnel problems since the lion's share of most academic budgets is tied up in salaries and fringe benefits for faculty and staff. On an overall scale, many deans and provosts find themselves either with too many people, too few people, or the wrong kinds of people in the wrong places trying to do the wrong things. The mismatch is often the result of changing institutional missions, priorities, and student interests. Whatever the causes, experienced deans and provosts know that if they had the right people in the right places doing the right things, many of their other problems would go away or be significantly reduced in severity.

On the individual and personal scale, people problems consume a great deal of the dean's and provost's time and contribute significantly to their anxieties. Since people who work at colleges and universities are usually quite bright, highly specialized and trained, and deeply committed to particular points of view, it is inevitable that misunderstandings and conflicts arise. The case studies in this chapter deal with some examples of these kinds of difficulties.

The Unauthorized Job Offer

One of the difficulties likely to occur involves the department chair or head who has exceeded his or her authority in speaking with candidates for faculty positions. The dean or provost walks a fine line in encouraging department chairs to be aggressive in recruiting faculty and in reminding them that several things have to be checked out "up the line" before commitments can be made. The following case study presents the kind of difficulties that can arise when a chair preempts the hiring process.

CASE STUDY

At Central College, Dean Cranston's rush toward completion of the promotion recommendations was interrupted by his assistant. He had told her of his need to finish the promotions and knew that something important (and probably ominous) must be at hand for her to intrude in this way. His apprehension was confirmed when she said the phone call had to do with the search for the new faculty member in art history.

The caller was the chair of the art history department at Southeastern, a well-known and respected state university. He asked why one of his graduate students had been offered a position, only to have the offer subsequently withdrawn. As the dean listened in growing disbelief, it appeared that Joe Smith, the art chair at Central, had gone out of his way two weeks ago to assure the applicant from Southeastern that he would indeed be offered the position and that only paperwork formalities remained.

The reality was that the search committee had ultimately recommended two other candidates to the dean and the dean had extended an offer to one of them—an offer subsequently accepted. Now, with the position filled, the dean wondered, first, why the chair hadn't informed him of his outstanding verbal offer. Beyond that, the dean was puzzled by the apparent breakdown of communication between the chair, the committee, and himself. Finally, a frown crossed his face as he recalled the college attorney's presentation at deans' council about court awards based on verbal contracts. The chair, the dean mused, must have felt confident at first of his own choice and later realized that he had overreached himself. At any rate, the dean's speculations were pushed aside when he heard the Southeastern chair asking what Central was prepared to do for his student.

The dean assured the chair at Southeastern that he would check the situation out thoroughly and get back to him later that same day. It looked like he'd have to work on the promotions that evening after the faculty senate meeting. Right now, he had to contact his art department chairman.

Assuming that the facts all check out—that is, his chair did indeed make a firm offer unguarded by the usual "pending approval by so and so"—Dean Cranston clearly has two problems—internal and external.

How would you advise him to proceed with them?

Response # 1

Dean Cranston's difficulties are due to a number of failures, at least one very much his own. Why, in the name of all academic reason, would he move to confirm an appointment without first telling the chair? He is rightly distressed that the chair didn't tell him about the early verbal offer, but in view of all the circumstances it is going to be impossible for him to get very righteously indignant about it. There is plenty of mea culpa to go around, and occasions for many embarrassed explanations. The problem, however, remains.

Assuming that the higher administration is unwilling to honor both "appointments" fully, or to consider a ready cash buyout of the Southeastern student's arguable property interest, there appear to be only two possibilities, which should be explored serially. The dean, with his mouth full of humble pie, should first lay out the whole sorry mess and ask collective forgiveness. If that doesn't work, it is likely very promptly to become a legal matter.

Without knowing more than the case provides about the laws and precedents regarding contracts in Dean Cranston's state, and about the established formal process of confirming appointments at Central College, it is impossible to predict what the college's chances would be as defendant in a lawsuit. Evidently, the college attorney would not be sanguine about it, and in the way of attorneys would therefore urge some kind of negotiated settlement if it appeared that the disappointed Southeastern student seemed really serious about prosecution. All told, that might be the best solution, painful though it would be in light of the gleeful attention likely to be given it by the press.

However that part of it turned out, the dean, as noted, has a couple of critical internal problems. The response to one of them is easy: All chairs should be firmly, clearly, and in writing informed that offers of this kind are absolutely verboten, and this admonition should be made clear to all new chairs as they appear. The other problem, because it is his own, is harder. He should make no excuses and put no greater blame on his chairs than he takes upon himself—who, after all, is the one who would be most expected to know better. He can hope that his vice president, president, and board are understanding and forgiving—at least once. But he should resolve right now to quit deaning if he is ever unfortunate enough to make a similar mistake again. (George R. Healy, retired, former Provost, College of William and Mary, Williamsburg, Virginia.)

Response #2

Indeed, Dean Cranston does have both an external problem and an internal problem. It is obvious that Central should honor the commitment he made; thus, the position is filled. Barring some very innovative way of removing this applicant (the dean's choice) from the field, we are left with no alternative but to conclude that no position exists for the Southeastern graduate (the chair's choice).

A first step in dealing with the external problem might be to investigate the possibility of finding resources to employ both persons. Since this is remote, the dean should explain to the graduate student, "We're sorry; the position is already filled. At the time that he talked to you, the department chair did not know that the position was already committed" (or "didn't follow procedures," whichever is accurate). This assumes the dean's authority to assign positions takes precedence over the department chair's authority. We might even raise the question as to whether the chair has any such authority at all. If both have such authority to act independently of each other, then Central College really has an awkward internal situation that needs immediate clarification. If only the dean has authority to make such final com-

mitments, then there is less likelihood of a successful legal challenge.

Internally, the incident should be used as a learning experience for the entire institution. It would entail clarifying procedures and stressing the urgency of accurate and complete communications, thus providing a sufficient "slap on the wrist" to the
chair for making the unauthorized offer—if, indeed, it is unauthorized.

This is a no-win situation. It does not provide the luxury of
face-saving maneuvers for the chair. (N. Gayle Simmons, Executive Vice President, Central Piedmont Community College,
Charlotte, North Carolina.)

Both responses point to the awkwardness of the situation and
the unlikelihood that face-saving measures can be found. The first
response (Provost Healy) explores some of the legal problems and
lays the culpability squarely on the dean. This is something more
than the usual, "When the chairs err, it's the dean's fault because
it's the dean's responsibility to instruct the chairs adequately."
Here we are dealing with a serious error in the modus operandi
of the dean himself. The second response (Executive Vice President Simmons) has the dean carrying the bad news to the Southeastern student, and urges that the incident become a learning
experience for the entire institution. In both responses, it is clear
that additional internal clarification is needed.

In these situations, it is likely that the chair's assurances were
presented optimistically and received as more definitive than intended. Few people like to convey bad news and often couch it
in the most favorable and therefore misleading light. Provosts,
deans and chairs need periodically to remind themselves of the
A-B-C's: accuracy, brevity and clarity.

What Do You Do with an Alcoholic Dean?

Because of the highly talented and highly motivated types of persons colleges and universities hire, and because of the pressures
and tensions of the work they do, it should not come as a surprise
that there are problems with alcoholism and drugs among faculty,

chairs, deans, provosts, and other officers. The increase of various forms of chemical dependency in society at large during recent years adds to but doesn't change the nature of the problem.

Some forms of chemical dependency are technically classified as diseases and so are "protected" categories in terms of laws barring discrimination. However, inadequate performance is not a protected category, and most institutions can tolerate only so much. Academic administrators must find ways of dealing with the latter while humanely trying to do something effective about the former. The following case study explores some of the difficulties involved in these matters.

CASE STUDY

The three department chairs who sat in Provost Janice Everready's outer office had come for some answers. They first came as a group two weeks ago to explain that their dean had become a visible alcoholic. In spite of their high regard for him and what he had been able to do during his decade as dean, the chairs admitted that they were finally at their wits' end in trying to cover up for him.

The problem had started only a year ago, shortly after the dean's son was killed in an automobile accident. Most people who had witnessed his excessive drinking wrote it off as a normal response to such a severe trauma. Everyone expected that in due course the dean would take hold again and that his drinking would revert to its normal social level. The chairs had come two weeks ago to say that it hadn't happened and to offer their support to the provost in dealing with the matter.

Everready, of course, had heard about the worsening problem before the chairs confronted her with it. She had made some discreet inquiries to get a firmer fix on the seriousness of the problem. She had decided that the chairs were right. The time for action was at hand.

What kind of action should Everready take?

Response # 1

The death of the dean's son puts a special gloss on this case by heightening the need for consideration and sensitivity toward the dean. Nevertheless, when a drinking problem has manifestations that affect his job performance, action should be firm, clear, and certain.

Everready should confront the dean with the complaints heard and behaviors observed (though maintaining confidentiality of sources) and be guided by the dean's response.

If the dean admits to a drinking problem, assistance should be offered through a leave of absence, independent counseling, and periodic reviews of his condition up to a certain date. At that time, and if rehabilitation fails, additional steps could be taken, ranging from consideration of medical disability, early retirement, or forced resignation.

Should the dean deny the allegation, Everready should strongly suggest immediate resignation to avert a formal inquiry. Everready should also indicate that proceedings will be initiated to challenge the dean's tenure status. Everready should give the dean no more than one or two days to consider the options.

In my own experience with alcoholic faculty or administrators, the individuals did not resist the opportunity either to resign or to accept assistance when confronted with the potential exposure. From the available facts in this case (the son's death, the relatively short period of alcohol abuse), I would expect that rehabilitative assistance would be gratefully accepted and be successful. (Milton Greenberg, Provost and Vice President for Academic Affairs, The American University, Washington, D.C.).

Response # 2

We know that Janice had heard about the worsening problem before the date of the second meeting with the chairs. However, we do not know that she was aware of the worsening problem before the first meeting on the subject two weeks earlier. It is therefore probable that her discreet inquiries, as well as the comments from the chairs, were events of only the last two weeks. There is no indication that Janice has conferred with the dean, and certainly no evidence of efforts on her part to assist him.

His decade of accomplishment and the tragic death of his son should convince the provost that even though the time for action was at hand, such action should be carefully planned and sympathetic. In a word, it should focus upon the dean's problems rather than upon the department chairs' problems at this particular time. Janice should therefore avoid any temptation to suspend or terminate the dean. First, she should confer with him and possibly with his family (we are not told what family remains). If, in her considered opinion, his present condition makes his presence at school intolerable, she should recommend that he go on sick leave and seek help, both to ameliorate the grief and control the alcoholic addiction. The odds are that he will accept this recommendation from her and will warmly receive her pledge of support for him. Anything less would be unconscionable at this stage. This is not the point of desperation; rather, it is only the beginning of a series of actions that would be appropriate for Janice. Clearly, the first of these should focus upon her efforts to assist and support the dean. Certainly he is worth saving. (N. Gayle Simmons, Executive Vice President, Central Piedmont Community College, Charlotte, North Carolina.)

Response # 3

The objective is to attempt to save an individual troubled by alcohol—whether a dean, a faculty member, or any other person— and to see him or her restored to a productive life rather than destroyed. In this case, the dean has performed ably for a decade and has developed a drinking problem as a result of the death of a son.

One question to be asked is why Janice Everready had not already taken some action. Apparently, she was aware of the problem but had decided to do nothing until the chairs brought her a mandate for action. Thus, she placed herself in a reactive rather than proactive position.

Be that as it may, what should she do? The first step is a conference with the dean to discuss with him the perceptions of a drinking problem. If he denies the problem (a very high probability), Everready must be prepared to cite hard facts as evidence. These discussions are sensitive, and the dean should be reassured that the institution truly wants to help.

If the dean continues to deny the problem, the vice president must warn him that if he does not seek help, he will be removed from the dean's position and quite possibly from his tenured faculty position if the necessary hearings support the charge. Hopefully, at this point, the dean will submit either to counseling and/ or hospitalization. Obviously, a medical leave would be in order.

If he continues to deny the problem, Everready should demand the following: (1) The dean must submit to a full physical exam, paid for by the institution, if possible; (2) if no physical basis is detected to explain the problem, the dean must submit to a battery of psychological tests, also paid for by the institution; and (3) after these tests, if the institution is still convinced of the problem, the dean must seek help or be removed. If the dean refuses all three demands, removal should be immediate and the dean's department consulted about a return to the faculty or removal for cause from the faculty position.

Hopefully, faced with these choices, the dean will admit to the problem and seek help. If he does, Everready should not remove him pending the outcome of the counseling and/or hospitalization. A medical leave should be granted and the associate dean should serve as interim dean. (Thomas B. Brewer, Vice President for Academic Affairs, Georgia State University, Atlanta, Georgia.)

Each of the responses suggests conferring with the dean as a first step. It is important that this first step not be delayed. The dean is at risk of doing something while "under the influence" that could change the nature of the case and cast a long shadow over the rest of his career. While many pressing matters usually crowd a provost's or vice president's calendar, and although the conversation with the dean might be difficult, the temptation to put the matter off must be strenuously resisted. It's best to engage such situations immediately. This is one of those "do it today" matters.

As the responses suggest, the provost's discussion with the dean should start with comments on the dean's unsatisfactory performance, not with accusations of alcohol abuse. It can be argued that the primary issue here is one of performance unless and until the dean admits his own concerns about alcohol. Once this admission occurs, offers of assistance are more likely to be well received.

The Student Complaint

Issues once known primarily as matters of basic fairness, or even simply taste, have now been recognized as carrying important legal implications. The whole area of sexual harassment has been determined legislatively to violate individual rights. The frequent clear cases are surrounded by a profusion of ambiguous situations. These are often complicated by traditions of academic courtesy and debatable understandings of academic freedom. The following case study illustrates some of these complications.

CASE STUDY

Jean Dreyer was in her third year as arts and sciences dean at a large, comprehensive, urban university. Things had been running smoothly and she was enjoying her administrative responsibilities. The chairs were generally supportive and she was working well with the academic vice president. Her duties seemed manageable and she had even been able to keep up with some of her research.

In fact, she had just been thinking of her good fortune when a very agitated sophomore student entered her office. Mary Smith had requested the appointment yesterday but had not been clear about the reason. As Jean listened to Mary's rush of words, it became clear that Dr. Wilson was the reason.

An associate professor with sturdy credentials, Wilson had come to the institution in the fall with a reputation as a promising economist and an outspoken conservative. Dreyer had felt pleased at hiring him last spring, for she and the economics chair had hoped to upgrade the research profile of the department as well as to promote a diversity of viewpoints.

Mary said she had no quarrel with the importance of research or the value of a diversity of viewpoints. She had learned a lot from Wilson, and she was sure that others in the class had also. It was good for them to be challenged on issues like the ERA and equal pay for comparable work. She had realized the poverty of some of her earlier positions, and been forced to reconstruct some of her basic arguments. All of that was good.

What rankled, however, was the way Dr. Wilson seemed to denigrate the importance of women as scholars or entrepreneurs. He appeared to go out of his way to downplay their contributions nationally, and had even referred to various "bimbos" in the financial community. The course material made no reference to

women, and in his classroom lectures Wilson seemed to play to
the large number of men students with witty double-entendres
and off-color anecdotes. He just did not appear to take the women
students seriously.

She had thought about talking directly to Wilson, Mary continued, but was apprehensive about incurring his displeasure.
She didn't want to get a reputation as a malcontent and she needed
good grades for graduate school. She had seen the department
chair, but he had been of no help—telling her that she needed
first to talk with Wilson before he could take any action. It was
not only she who was upset, Mary added, for several other women
were also offended. They had held an impromptu meeting after
class yesterday and selected Mary as spokesperson, urging her
to see the dean at the earliest possible time.

Dean Dreyer knew as she listened to Mary that the vague
language in the institution's sexual harassment policy statement
wasn't going to be of much help. She also remembered the strenuous effort several people had put forward to get even the brief
policy statement approved and promulgated. The statement
stopped short of specifying sanctions and processes.

Mary was rather insistent that something be done and that
her identity be protected. How should the dean respond?

Response # 1

Dean Dreyer's problem would be simpler if all she needed to do
were to educate Wilson to the nonsexist culture of the university.
Unfortunately, her problem is the more complex one of also having to work to change the culture of the university to a less sexist
mode. With this complaint against Wilson, she has both the opportunity and the responsibility to do so.

The dean and the chair are both correct in their reluctance
to act upon what are—as long as Mary refuses to allow her name
to be used—essentially anonymous complaints. Mary's identity
cannot be protected. However, both Mary and the other students
need to raise the issues of sex bias and harassment in an atmosphere of neutrality where someone has the authority to take action if necessary. By meeting already with Wilson's department
chair and with the dean, Mary has called attention to the potential
for retribution by Wilson and thereby provided herself with a

measure of protection. And if, indeed, Wilson does not take women in his class seriously, she has little reason to believe that she would, in any event, receive particularly outstanding grades from him. Assured that Mary has relatively little to lose, Dean Dreyer should set up a meeting between Wilson and Mary, with the department chair acting as a mediator, in order to allow Mary to air her grievances and those of the other women students in Wilson's classes.

Mary should be advised to be as specific as possible in her complaints, to cite instances and cases, and to avoid personalities. Wilson should be given an opportunity to respond, and the chair should be charged with the responsibility of making a recommendation to the dean after hearing all the evidence as well as Wilson's response. If Wilson's attitudes are indeed as Mary describes them, the chair undoubtedly is already aware of them to some extent, and Wilson is bound to display them in the meeting with Mary and the chair. Since the institution's harassment policy is too weak to hang anything (or anyone) on, the dean's actions must be based upon whatever general standards of academic fairness do exist in the institution.

It is particularly important that this case be handled in an informal and collegial manner, at least at the outset. A well-publicized sexual harassment case would not benefit the university, and Dean Dreyer has nothing to gain from directly antagonizing Wilson. Moreover, the lack of a strong institutional policy here really limits the actions she can take. Her role must be that of an educator, not a police officer. (David Seligman, Associate Dean of Faculty, Skidmore College, Saratoga Springs, New York.)

Response # 2

Since the issues Mary has presented are complex and could have far-reaching consequences, Dean Dreyer would do best to listen carefully during this first session, while saying little. She will, however, want to ask a few factual questions and attempt to get some sense of the group Mary is representing and of the young woman herself. She will also want to reassure Mary that it was quite proper for her to come in to talk, at the same time as she explains to her the potential gravity of such charges. She will ask Mary to put the account in writing, simply and straightforwardly, and will promise to protect her identity until and unless Mary herself releases her from that commitment. If Mary refuses to put the matter in writing, Dean Dreyer will have to indicate that she cannot proceed without even that much from a complainant. If Mary agrees to go ahead, they should set a time for a subsequent meeting in the near future.

Assuming that Mary decides to make a statement, and perhaps even to obtain the signatures of some of the other concerned students, the dean should move quickly to discuss the case—without mentioning names—with the academic vice president and the university's affirmative action officer, if one exists. She will want to reread the existing policy on sexual harassment to see whether it might, after all, provide for some sanctions or procedures. With or without the latter, she will want to prepare at least a tentative plan of action before her next session with Mary.

During this second meeting, the dean will want to show Mary that she is actually bringing several distinct charges, which must be differentiated from each other if appropriate remedies are to be sought. These charges, as I see them, are as follows: (1) Professor Wilson's course materials do not incorporate scholarship about or by women; (2) Professor Wilson does not take women students seriously, and actually favors the men in the class; and (3) Professor Wilson's class presentations include double entendres and off-color anecdotes.

Since the first allegation concerns the course curriculum, it should be dealt with separately. The dean may at that point choose to talk about academic freedom, its importance, and the difficult issues it raises. She will no doubt also want to admit, however regretfully, that gender-balancing the curriculum tends to be a slow process, its slowness not restricted to Professor Wilson's courses alone. Having said that, she should also assure Mary that as arts and sciences dean she will take the responsibility for raising these curricular issues with both Professor Wilson and the department chairperson as bearing on curricular currency and completeness, as well as on the importance of balanced points of view about major issues.

The dean should then explain that she sees the remaining allegations—those concerning unequal treatment of students and offensive language—as possibly being grounds for a charge of sexual harassment. She will want to talk about the gravity of such charges, but also emphasize the student's right to make them if she is convinced of her case. She will also have to tell Mary that any further steps will involve revealing her identity, though it will be possible to protect her and others bringing charges against retaliatory measures. At this point, the dean will have to walk a delicate line between presenting the whole matter as serious, while at the same time giving Mary the support to follow her honest convictions. She may want to encourage Mary to discuss all this with the group she is representing. They, too, will become part of the process, if they are bringing charges, and they may wind up directly involved in formal or informal hearings. Mary must also be told what procedures are likely to follow the formal harassment charge. Since federal law mandates investigation of all such allegations, the university's inadequate policies make appropriate continuation of the case more difficult, but in no way bar its pursuit.

The absence of agreed-upon university procedures means that these will now have to be developed on an ad hoc basis if Mary, with or without her companions, wishes to carry the matter forward. Dean Dreyer might meet again with the academic vice president to suggest that he establish a task force to develop a hearing procedure for this particular case, as well as more permanent published procedures. Given federal legislation, the university does not have the luxury of ignoring allegations of harassment, and even the most reluctant faculty members will quickly understand the advantage of procedures that are neither ad hoc nor ad hominem.

There is one more step that the dean, with the agreement of the vice president (and the shadowy affirmative action officer) should take. It is to ask Mary, any of her classmates who wish to join her, Professor Wilson, and the latter's department chairperson to meet with her in an attempt to resolve the case informally. Of course, the dean will first have to meet separately with the professor and the chairperson to explain the allegations made and the intent of the meeting. Should Professor Wilson or Mary refuse to attend such a session, nothing else can be done until the task force has developed its procedures and these have been approved at the highest levels of the university administration.

If Dean Dreyer succeeds in bringing the parties together in her office, she will have to guide the exchange very carefully and make sure that all there understand the purpose of the session: to allow the student(s) to share her (their) grievances with the professor and to give the latter a chance to respond in his own behalf. It is especially important that students and professor hear each other. Professor Wilson is in his first year at the university: Might he be unfamiliar with a coeducational classroom? Now that his attention has been drawn to his witticisms, does he himself consider them appropriate to a classroom? Can he see how they might offend women students and, one hopes, men as well? Did the women, perhaps, misunderstand his words or intentions? Can he identify any of his actions that might lead women students to feel discriminated against in class? It should be all too obvious that this exchange can misfire at any point, degenerate into a shouting match, or come to an abrupt end as one or another of the participants refuses to continue.

Assuming that all goes well, so that the various points of view have been explored to whatever extent seems possible, the dean must undertake the difficult task of summing up and of turning attention to the future. Is Mary, are her companions, satisfied that their concerns have been heard? Will Professor Wilson undertake to exercise care in the future, to avoid all behavior that might give rise to suspicions of preference, neglect, or harassment? Does either party wish to request additional formal steps? If not, the dean may declare the matter closed. Though a record of the meeting will be kept in her files, along with the complaint, none of this will be referred to again unless similar charges against Professor Wilson were to be brought in the future. With a great sigh of relief, Dean Dreyer can thank the chairperson for his help and acknowledge both Mary's and Professor Wilson's professional demeanor in a very difficult situation. She can then go home and brew herself a good strong cup of tea or mix herself a good stiff drink. She deserves it! (Ursula Colby, Academic Dean, Russell Sage College, Troy, New York.)

Both responses recognize the need to settle this matter informally if possible. The first response (Dean Seligman) lays out the nature of a meeting to be called by the dean to attempt such an informal resolution. The second response (Dean Colby) further describes how this meeting should be conducted. While it is clear that such meetings add substantially to the anxiety burden of deans and provosts, we can all be encouraged by the realization that these informal and personal efforts to resolve difficult situations work most of the time. Such is the magic of deaning.

The Protester

Extramural political involvements and utterances can generate delicate and sticky issues for deans and provosts. On the one hand, professors enjoy constitutional freedom of speech. On the other hand, there are certain responsibilities that come with being a professor and a member of an intellectual community. Matters can become difficult when a faculty member becomes so absorbed in an issue that his or her other work becomes secondary.

Additional difficulties arise when the issue taken up is controversial among broad portions of the academic community as well as the community beyond. If the professor's actions and utterances are offensive to important local or state authorities, or if they result in withdrawal of significant financial support from the institution by influential alumni, the dean and/or provost is likely to hear about it and become personally involved. The following case presents some of the elements likely to arise in these types of situations.

CASE STUDY

The provost could hear the chants through the closed window and he knew without even looking that Professor Howard Amster would be in the front row. He didn't need the student protesters or Howard Amster to tell him that apartheid was an ugly, repugnant, and unacceptable form of social ordering. For that matter, he had not needed Amster's earlier stridency over the issue of the proper treatment of laboratory research animals or his angry letters to the editor of the city newspaper denouncing the plans to establish a center for Islamic studies at the university.

Amster, however, seemed determined to be in the forefront of protest efforts, even though his own teaching and research accomplishments were suffering as a result. This was the year he was to finish his book, but there was little likelihood that he would, given the energy he was pouring into the protests. That would be unfortunate. The provost had seen the chair's earlier evaluation of Amster and had added his own warning, stressing the importance of scholarly accomplishments for a positive tenure decision.

Provost Clarke appreciated Amster's moral conviction, but was beginning to be concerned about the judiciousness of the influence he seemed to be exercising on the students. The trustees had made it very clear, he thought, that they would not divest the endowment of stocks of companies dealing in South Africa simply for the sake of divestment. Before the trustees' decision there had been open forums on campus, with debate and question-and-answer sessions. Some of the student concerns had indeed been met and prospects for a fairly good atmosphere established. From what he had been told, though, it appeared that Amster was continuing to agitate the students, having reportedly called the forum meetings a whitewash of racist attitudes.

There were several substantial alumni gifts in the works, the president had told him yesterday, and the president did not want them jeopardized by Amster's conduct. Neither, Clarke knew, would the president want the institution to be seen as pro-apartheid. The provost was afraid that Amster might be successful in creating that impression if the institution were to take any overt action against him or the protesters.

The provost's musings on what to do were interrupted by his secretary's voice, informing him that the president was on the phone and wanted his counsel on the issue. How should he advise the president and what should he do about Amster?

Response # 1

Amster may or may not have made a conscious choice to give up the possibility of finishing his book in opting to raise his voice in protest over social and political issues. Certainly, having already been warned by the chair of the importance of scholarly accomplishments for a positive tenure decision, he is aware of the potential consequences. It may be that he has reached a dead end with his research or lost interest in the project. Perhaps he realizes that the more stridently political he becomes, the more difficult it will be to deny him tenure without at least raising the possibility in many minds that he is being silenced. Moreover, any attempts at friendly advice from the provost will undoubtedly be seen by Amster as implied threats from the administration in violation of his academic freedom and freedom of speech. But, clearly, the president feels under pressure to do something. Unfortunately, neither the provost nor the president has many options. So long as Amster acts within the law and the institution's own rules, no disciplinary action can be taken.

The trustees' decision not to divest was made on the basis of the campus forums. If there are respectable voices (including Amster's) on campus arguing that the forums were not an adequate basis for the trustees' decision, perhaps the matter can be examined more fully. After all, the situation in South Africa is constantly changing. Now, a year after the original decision, it might be time to take another look. Provost Clarke should advise the president to create a blue-ribbon campus task force on divestment and appoint Amster to it, making certain that the composition of the task force is well-balanced and reputable with both faculty and trustees. Given the current state of campus agitation, the trustees should have no trouble agreeing to the creation of such a group—and indeed of being represented on its membership— and concerned faculty and students would certainly welcome the opportunity to voice their concerns in a forum in which they might have genuine influence.

The provost should then congratulate Amster on his appointment (copy to the department chair) and add his hopes that the additional responsibilities will not detract from Amster's goal of completing his book and meeting his other responsibilities as a faculty member. Assuming that the institution has a faculty tenure and promotions committee, the provost will be in a position simply to endorse without comment the inevitable tenure denial. The president and provost can expect a most unpleasant year of appeals and possibly suits—or worse, a year of bitter agitation—from a disaffected Amster on terminal appointment, and they might begin now to consider ways to minimize the impact. (David Seligman, Associate Dean of Faculty, Skidmore College, Saratoga Springs, New York.)

Response # 2

The president is on the phone. Thinking time is over. Provost Clarke should show the president the need to inform the alumni donors in detail and in writing of what he has done about the issue of apartheid. The president should be advised to send the alumni newspaper clippings and a full accounting of the protest events and open forums on the campus. The president should

explain to the donors—in an open letter in the alumni magazine—
what the issues are. A series of essays in the alumni magazine by
the faculty—Professor Howard Amster should be asked to write—
for and against, representing all possible campus views, and a
series by the students will show the academic community doing
what it should do—thinking and asking questions, then acting
according to those thoughts.

The next problem is what to do about Amster? The provost
needs to write an *aide-mémoire* outlining formally the importance
of scholarly accomplishments for a positive tenure decision. The
chair of Amster's department should write one as well. In addition,
I would advise the provost to ask the dean to interview those
members of the faculty who will be coming up for tenure in the
next few years. This should be a genuinely formative interview
in which each faculty member discusses his or her plans for development in their teaching and scholarly work. What are they
doing? What is the intellectual question their book is answering?
Why was that question of interest to them? What will come next?
How would they describe their teaching style? What do they like
best about teaching? What do they expect the university to be?
How will they contribute personally to the development of their
expectations of the university?

A hidden piece of the agenda in the case of Amster is to try
and find out why he is avoiding his scholarly work and risking
his career—a career he clearly values. Is he unconsciously trying
to set up a scenario in which others can be blamed for his own
failure? Or is he a prophetic type who would be honored even
as he is told that prophets rarely get tenure? (Eva Hooker, Vice
President for Academic Affairs, Saint John's University, Collegeville, Minnesota.)

Response # 3

Angry shouts and chants reverberating through closed windows
are, indeed, fear-inducing, and readily conjure images of faceless
mobs in Teheran and elsewhere. One's initial sympathies thus
lean toward Provost Clarke, caught between an alarmed president,
upset—perhaps outraged—students, and a faculty member whose
rights must be respected, according to the rules of the academic
game, but who may not himself be too scrupulous in this respect
vis-à-vis others. Nonetheless, careful scrutiny of the case suggests

that Provost Clarke may have allowed himself to become excessively alarmed and may be in some danger of losing his grip on the central values to be protected.

For one thing, stridency in defense of animal rights and a letter to the editor of the local newspaper protesting a university decision are not particularly marks of a man given to extreme or violent behavior. Furthermore, the wording of the case—e.g., [concern about] "the judiciousness of the influence he *seemed* to be exercising on the students" (my emphasis)—suggests the absence of proof that Professor Amster is actually responsible for the chanting, much less for inciting students to illegal, seriously disruptive, or violent behavior. It is not, in any case, a part of the academic tradition that a professor's influence on students necessarily appear "judicious" in the view of administrators.

Thus, the provost's fear that Amster might be able to create an impression that the university is pro-apartheid, were there to be overt action against him, seems misplaced, since there appears in any case to be no present basis for such action. Professor Amster is well-protected by both the First Amendment and the traditions of academic freedom. Provost Clarke, on the other hand, might do well to consider what the university's disregard for these protections could do to its image.

Were the provost to arrive at conclusions similar to these, he might consider inviting Professor Amster to come and talk about the situation. Assuming that Clarke kept away from all subjects having to do with Amster's unfinished book and his prospects for tenure, such a conversation could allow both men to gain some insight into each other's motivations and final objectives. The provost could try to share with the professor his own sense of the directions in which the university has begun to move, and could seek to communicate his evident conviction that lower-keyed strategies might be surer ways of moving the board toward eventual disinvestment than pressure for abrupt decisions. At worst, the face-to-face exchange would accomplish nothing. At best, it might even be possible for the provost to make the case for continued open debate, allowing many voices to be heard, many positions to be analyzed. Perhaps the professor could be brought to a renewed awareness of the real importance of *these* freedoms in the education of American and world citizens.

Whatever the outcome of such a meeting, the provost will have to pursue other avenues as well. His words to the professor about open debate must be no mere rhetoric. In fact, he will have to devote major energies to encouraging student leaders, faculty, and others in the university to widen and deepen the debates about apartheid and divestiture. It should be his special responsibility to make sure that the campus as well as the community have access to as many facts and points of view as possible in relation to these issues. It will be important, for example, to get students and others thinking about the complex responsibilities of trustees exercising a fiduciary role, as well as about different theories on the economic impact of divestiture on different populations in South Africa. The dissemination of facts and the keen analysis of issues would seem to be considerably more appropriate to an academic community's attempt to make difficult ethical decisions than chanting.

His musings abruptly terminated by the telephone, the provost must now find the words to persuade the president to agree to the values and strategies he is proposing. He will need to calm fears, while admitting that the situation, if not defused, could turn ugly in the future. Provost Clarke will want to urge the president to set aside other considerations and to ponder for a few minutes the critical importance to any university of open debate and peaceful assembly. He will want to suggest that infringing on these is far more likely to harm the university's image than faculty stridency or student zeal. The president must be brought to invest the dignity and authority of his office in carrying this message to disgruntled alumni. Provost and president should work together to create a context allowing students to become educated participants in the university's continued struggle to resolve complex issues—responsibly, rationally, and humanely. (Ursula Sybille Colby, Academic Dean, Russell Sage College, Troy, New York.)

Each of the responses calls for involving the protesting professor in further discussion. The first response (Dean Seligman) suggests including him in a blue-ribbon task force. The second response (Vice President Hooker) sees him writing essays for the alumni magazine. The third response (Dean Colby) envisions discussions between Amster and the provost. It is interesting to note that all three call for more discussion in the face of the trustees' determination that discussion was over.

A difficult issue for deans and provosts is determining when a closed subject is really closed. The academic tradition is to re-open everything again and again and again. It is entirely possible that the president's phone call is to advise the provost that the chairman of the board has just called and made it clear that he wants the ruckus stopped. The president and the provost know that it can't be stopped, as do the three respondents.

Trustees generally have little patience with campus unrest of any kind. One can almost hear the anger in the admonition from one or more of the trustees, "Mr. President, you're *supposed* to be in charge and we . . ." Just as it only takes one Amster to continue agitation, it may take only one determined trustee to convince *his* colleagues that a decision has been made and further discussion is intolerable and an insult to their authority as a board. Presidencies have fallen over such matters.

Before any strategy is undertaken to continue, contain, or re-solve the campus situation, there may have to be very serious discussions between the president and the board. If those dis-cussions yield a definitive result, the provost may have to fall into line with it or move on.

Amster has plenty of protections. The president and provost do not.

Faculty Intimacy

Faculty members are in unusual positions of trust. Students rely on them for guidance in a wide variety of areas and look to them for role models. Consequently, the relationship between faculty members and students is, or can become, quite close. Perhaps only the relationships between doctors, lawyers, and ministers with those they serve offer greater opportunities for sharing and greater potential for abuse of the confidence necessary to the re-lationship. Some faculty believe that changing societal mores have altered the character of these relationships and that liberties or intimacies once commonly ruled inappropriate are now more matters of individual choice. Others, though, will contend that changing mores have not changed the requirements of true professionalism. Both points of view are present on most campuses and, given time, deans and provosts become caught up in them, as the next case study shows.

CASE STUDY

The rumors about Joel Cohen had been quiet, but persistent. A middle-aged professor of psychology, Cohen had for years been associated in the local gossip with a string of attractive, young coeds. Every other year or so there seemed to be a new one, taking up residence in Cohen's townhouse and accompanying him to occasional college social activities. Cohen had apparently been reasonably discreet, for the provost had not earlier received any complaints. She had not personally approved of this apparent serial promiscuity, but had gone to some lengths to keep her personal value judgments separate from her professional assessments of Cohen's teaching and research accomplishments.

Now, however, with Sarah, Cohen's personal life had spilled over dramatically into his college responsibilities. Like her predecessors, Sarah had apparently been mesmerized initially by Cohen's personal charm and his teaching abilities. She had continued enrolling in his classes after moving in with him, and within a year had become his teaching assistant. No one was quite sure what had precipitated things, but a month ago Sarah and Cohen had had a violent exchange at a faculty cocktail party. She had apparently moved out that night, and now her letter of complaint and accusation were on the provost's desk.

The charges were blunt enough. Infuriated by her rejection of him, Cohen had taken gross advantage of his faculty position and—so Sarah alleged—out of spite had flunked her on the capstone department course as well as on the independent study course she had had with him. Additionally, he was refusing to provide her any professional references. The department chair was a good friend of Cohen's, she added, and had been of no help when she complained, telling her instead that she should take her complaint first to Cohen.

Hence, her letter concluded, the need to appeal to the provost. Cohen, she charged, had displayed extremely unprofessional behavior in his conduct toward her, and she wanted him reprimanded, if not indeed fired. She had not realized earlier, but she understood now—and she should have known all along—how inappropriate it was for a professor to accept his or her lover as a student in a class.

Supporting letters from three women professors had also come in the morning mail, each arguing that the institution should do something to discourage such relationships between faculty and students—that more often than not, they were harmful to women students and that in any case they were unprofessional abuses of privilege and station by the faculty. Looking at the letters, the provost pondered how to respond and how to prevent similar situations in the future.

How would you advise her?

Response # 1

Cases like this are powerful reminders that an academic community is first of all a human community. Both how we deal with them and how well we deal with them can have a powerful influence on the well-being and reputation of the entire institution. Trying to resolve them effectively requires the time, energy, and concern to talk with people who are feeling a good deal of emotional stress. Clarifying issues and exploring options for resolving them is rarely a neat and prescribed process; statements of formal policies and procedures are therefore of limited value.

That is why I would recommend that the provost begin to deal with this problem by talking with Sarah. The purpose of that conversation would be twofold. First, Sarah should know that someone in authority at the institution cares about her situation and is willing to take the time to hear her perspectives on it. Not to do this—i.e., to allow Sarah to believe that no one will respond to her concern—is to create the potential for the problem to get much worse.

The second purpose of this conversation is to reach an agreement with Sarah about what follow-up actions will and will not be taken. If she is demanding that Cohen be fired immediately, the provost should tell her very clearly that this will not happen and explain why it will not happen. If Sarah insists that the provost get back to her about what actions have been taken by the institution regarding Cohen, the provost must decide whether she is willing to do that. If she is not, Sarah needs to know that as well. Essentially, the provost needs to think through what she will do next, decide what role, if any, Sarah will play in that strategy, and then communicate those intentions to Sarah.

The next step would be a meeting with Cohen. The provost should begin the conversation descriptively—i.e., indicating what Sarah has told her, without assuming that all of it is accurate, while also respecting any promises of confidentiality she made to Sarah. Cohen should then be invited to reply.

To whatever extent Sarah's story is true, Cohen needs to understand that he now has a serious problem. Of course, the institution also has a problem. But, Cohen does not have the freedom to say or feel, "It's not my problem." He may choose to recognize the problem, he may refuse to deal with it, but he has a problem nonetheless. As a representative of the institution that also has a problem because of Cohen's actions, the provost should make it clear that she intends to try to resolve the problem with or without his help. It is to everyone's benefit if it is with his help.

If Cohen is responsive to that, the next step becomes a matter of exploring ways in which the issue can be resolved. Is it possible and/or desirable to have a colleague evaluate Sarah's work with Cohen to support or challenge the determination of her failing grade? Such an option is probably unthinkable without Cohen's full consent and cooperation. Would a three-way meeting between Cohen, Sarah, and the provost be helpful? Can the department chair be helpful? Cohen and the provost should explore these options together and then agree upon next steps.

That, however, does not end the conversation. Cohen needs to know that he has another problem as a result of this situation. He needs to know that this issue has become a matter of concern to other members of the campus community and that three of his faculty colleagues have written to the provost to express their concern about this matter. Again, the issue becomes: What will Cohen and/or the provost do to address that problem?

The provost should be aware of at least two additional points. First, it might be wise to meet with the three female faculty members who wrote letters and ask them to discuss ways in which the faculty might address the issues raised by this situation. Perhaps a statement of faculty policy should be considered. The point here is that this is an excellent opportunity for the faculty to wrestle with a matter of professional behavior among themselves as professionals. While she will want to play a very active role in those discussions, the provost should be reluctant to let the faculty say to her, in effect, "Here, you deal with it." If they are concerned about it, it becomes a matter for them to deal with also.

Finally, while trying to resolve the problem in these ways and thereby recognizing that statements of policy are of limited value in dealing with them, the provost should also be careful not to violate the spirit or intent of whatever statements of policy or procedure apply. Regardless of what the provost and Cohen may do, Sarah always has the right to carry her grievance further. Thus, the provost should not put herself in the position of having violated the institution's due process.

Sarah and Cohen have handed the provost a very messy problem. Unfortunately, there is no neat, clean, and simple way adequately to resolve it. Rather, resolution depends upon the provost's human relations skills as well as the sense of respect that Cohen and Sarah have for her integrity. (Mark H. Collier, Vice President for Academic Affairs, Baldwin-Wallace College, Berea, Ohio.)

Response # 2

The provost of this institution needs to respond to the Joel Cohen affair promptly and vigorously, but always with tact and discretion. In doing so, she should accomplish four things: (1) gather as much information as possible from as many reliable sources as available; (2) based upon this information, establish clearly the issues to be addressed; (3) articulate for herself the possible courses of action and their ramifications concerning each of the issues identified; and (4) while being open and direct in gathering information from the parties involved and from others, employ the utmost discretion so as not to jeopardize any future action that may be necessary.

Few issues evoke as much sensitivity and emotion as those involving the possibility of moral turpitude. Given the recent attention to sexual harassment on the job as well as to behavioral ethics within the profession, the provost needs to act clearly and decisively, but only after gathering as much of the information as possible. She should begin by interviewing the student making the complaint. Then she should meet privately with Professor Cohen as soon as possible. The provost must clarify to both parties that open and frank discussion of the issues is essential. She should also make it clear that she would welcome further information or the names of possible witnesses or other interested parties. The purpose of these initial discussions is not to resolve blame but to gather the facts.

It is necessary to repeat this last point consistently in order to reduce some of the emotional tension involved. The provost needs to separate the true facts of the case from the generalizations that will naturally develop. Vague implications and unsubstantiated related issues, while contributing to the atmosphere, may not necessarily bear upon this specific case. However, if those involved in similar situations in the past would wish to testify freely, they should be encouraged to do so. Under no circumstances, however, should they be coerced or be made to feel undue pressure.

Once the facts have been gathered, the provost will need to decide what specific issues to address. She must consider faculty ethics, undue prejudice, and even outright violations of established codes of behavior and conduct. In any case, the liability of the faculty member, or possibly of the student herself, may become a legal issue to which the provost needs to be atuned.

Most institutions generally recognize four grounds for dismissal of a tenured faculty member: professional incompetence, immoral conduct, neglect of duty or insubordination, and the discontinuance or reorganization of a program. It is possible that Professor Cohen may have placed his career in jeopardy in two of these areas—by his conduct, which may be considered immoral by his peers, and by his neglect of duty, considering the manner in which he is alleged to have graded Sarah's classroom performance. The second may be more difficult to establish. The first, however, relates to possible uninvited sexual advances to other students in the college. At this point, the provost must determine whether such advances were uninvited and unwelcomed. The student's complicity in the arrangement will naturally have a great deal of bearing on the definition of immoral conduct.

The next issue includes Professor Cohen's possible prejudices in evaluating Sarah's classroom performance. In this case, the student needs to take the initiative by following published guidelines for a grade appeal. It is the provost's responsibility to inform the student of her rights under this procedure and to assist her in understanding what kinds of evidence would be acceptable in such an appeal. Again, while an institutional mechanism in most cases has already been established to review the grade appeal, the information gathered by the provost concerning Sarah's possible complicity in the arrangement may have some bearing on whether the evidence provided by the student is believable and sound.

In determining the appropriate course of action, the provost must have identified the issues at stake and must be ready to show that the evidence presented has reasonable bearing upon her decisions. She must first consider the actions of the faculty member. Is sexual harassment truly involved, or is this simply a case of an adult affair gone awry? Secondly, are there any grounds for definition of moral turpitude? This definition implies a commonly accepted peer judgment against the actions of the faculty member. The AAUP "Statement on Procedural Standards in Faculty Dismissal Proceedings (1958)" indicated that ". . . in the effective college, a dismissal proceeding involving a faculty member on tenure or one occurring during the term of appointment, will be a rare exception, caused by individual human weakness and not by an unhelpful setting. . . . The faculty must be willing to recommend the dismissal of a colleague when necessary."

The second issue for which a course of action may be taken has to do with the unfair grading of the student. The faculty member may be liable where it can be shown that he or she deliberately and wrongfully gave a student a failing grade without sufficient reason. In such cases, the institution could be held blameless and the faculty member could be liable personally for any damages awarded. The provost should inform the faculty member clearly of this possibility to encourage a careful re-evaluation of the reasons for the failing grade being given. The student needs to initiate the grade appeal action should she indeed feel that she was prejudiced against. As indicated, most institutions have such a procedure, and the provost must tell the student clearly what courses of action are available to *her*. The department chair, having referred the student first to Professor Cohen, may have followed the letter of the requirement for student grievances at this institution. It does behoove the provost, however, to discuss the issue with the department chair to be certain that in this case there appears to be no cover-up or bias in the chair's action.

Finally, the provost must consider personal counseling for Cohen, Sarah, or both. Cohen defied the norms of discretion by most social standards. While not exactly relevant to this situation, the AAUP "Statement of Principles and Interpretive Comments on Academic Freedom and Tenure (1940)" indicates clearly that an instructor needs to show respect for "his special position in the community (which) imposes special obligations." Whether or not the provost has a case to recommend severe sanctions or dismissal, at least she has grounds for a strong reprimand and the giving of strong personal advice to the faculty member. If this is truly the first time that the issue has been raised directly with Professor Cohen, then the provost, all other evidence being uncertain, should invoke the strongest possible warning to him in the privacy of her office. In a separate conversation with the student, the provost must relay the gravity of the situation in which the student found herself, and without passing any blame needlessly, should warn the student of the pitfalls as well as the benefits she may face in pursuing any grievance.

The most difficult task for the provost will be dealing with the issue publicly. This will depend entirely upon the severity of the action taken. Should there be a formal hearing and a result of dismissal or censorship from this hearing, it is clear that a public announcement needs to be made, although the details of the case may remain private. If a reprimand has been given to the faculty member and the student elects not to file a grade appeal, then knowledge of this decision needs to be passed on not only to the faculty member and the student, but also to the department chair and the institution's president. At the very least, some form of apology from the faculty member to the student is in order to relieve the tensions.

It is my opinion that the provost has no formal obligation to nonparticipating interested outsiders who may have written supporting letters, unless that information has direct bearing as evidence in the case. The provost must retain an unbiased air in dealing with these matters unless the information gathered shows that strong positive action is not only warranted but truly helpful to all parties in the case.

To avoid similar situations in the future, the provost would be wise—depending upon what procedures, codes of conduct, and expectations have already been established by the faculty— to call for a review of what constitutes proper faculty conduct with students. This is a key strategy in making a public statement about the principles of an issue without involving any individual participants. The committee should include a cross-section of faculty, students, and administration, and should propose standards as well as penalties for any and all parties who take advantage of their situation in the profession, with or without complicity on the part of the students.

This final point is crucial. While from a legal point of view a student over the age of eighteen is an adult and is considered capable of making serious choices, within the educational environment an instructor has so much indirect power that a seemingly reasonable decision on the part of the student may be unwittingly prejudiced from the beginning. (Gregg Lacy, Dean of Academic Affairs, Keuka College, Keuka Park, New York.)

Both responses lay out an approach to this problem that proceeds from fact-finding toward various courses of action. The first response (Vice President Collier), while clearly indicating that there are no sure formulas for dealing with these situations, advises that immediate conversations should be held with the two parties directly involved. This is often the most difficult part of the process. It does, indeed, rely on the human relations skills of the provost. The second response (Dean Lacy) begins the same way and considers the possibilities surrounding dismissal for cause, concluding with the advisability of recommending personal counseling for one or both parties.

Swinging from a state of in loco parentis to one of almost complete laissez faire is within the memory of many faculty and administrators still guiding our institutions. This further complicates how these situations should be dealt with. Both respondents indicate that legal action may be just around the corner. In this litigious age, it may well be helpful for the provost involved to seek legal advice early in her considerations.

The last two decades have produced a body of case law that might bear on the situations described in this case study. Even the seemingly innocent matter of "fact-finding" is now surrounded by constraints that weren't there a while ago. This provost should avail herself of competent legal assistance lest she complicate matters by increasing the possibility that one or more of those involved might bring legal action against her as well as against the institution.

The committees called for to formulate possible definitions of acceptable faculty behavior might be impossible to organize on a campus where collective bargaining has led to the establishment of a contractual agreement between the faculty and the institution. It can be argued that such definitions bear upon the "conditions of employment" and are more appropriate to the bargaining table than to committee meetings.

In any case, the respondents are quite right in reminding us that these matters must be handled with discretion and an enormous amount of diplomacy. These attributes are not evenly distributed among the deans and provosts of the country. As a consequence, these matters generate a considerable amount of anxiety among those who have to handle them. Deans and provosts need personal support systems on their campuses or in their communities to help them deal with the stress generated by this kind of situation. Taking deliberate steps to insure that such support systems are available and at the ready has long been an important part of effective deaning.

──────CHAPTER FIVE──────
Dealing With Change

ALL ORGANIZATIONS change and evolve. Some do so rapidly; others at a barely perceptible pace. Even those that are seemingly quiescent are undergoing changes that will affect their future. True stasis is characteristic of death. Organizations, including academic organizations, are very much alive.

Although increasingly recognized as a constant, change makes most people uncomfortable. New courses of action contain unpredictable elements. These often conflict with the subtle sense of security that ensures an organization's continuation. However good or bad the organization's sense of itself might be, changes introduce new unknowns and carry the potential for making things either better or worse or both.

Academics have many reasons for greeting proposals for change with suspicion and reserve. They have long institutional memories and have seen many proposals come and go. Too often, they have seen that proposals having the potential to make things better don't work. Too often, those that do work have not resulted in improvement.

Having been trained to revere the old and constantly test and challenge the new, faculties are deeply shaped by a value system that mitigates against ready acceptance of change. Those who ridicule the conservatism of the academy and its renowned resistance to change would do well to consider the positive virtues inherent in testing, retesting, and testing again any proposal that suggests things might be done differently. There is merit in fidelity, being

125

true to a cause, and holding fast to that which one's training and experience has indicated to be of value. The oft-quoted witticism that changing a curriculum is like trying to move a cemetery might be a description of a blessing rather than a curse.

Yet anyone who has bothered to look at the history of higher education, or indeed the history of any single institution of higher education, soon comes to realize that change has characterized its institutional life and well-being. Because change is omnipresent and because academics are wary of its consequences, tensions abound in the academy. It is from these tensions that much of the institution's creativity arises. The case studies presented in this chapter deal with some of the difficulties inherent in dealing with change.

Introducing Merit Pay

Few subjects draw more discussion than that of setting and adjusting the faculty pay scale. Some believe that since all disciplines are—at least in an ideal world—of nearly equal value, so also are all practitioners of those disciplines. Others know that some work harder, as well as smarter, than others, and that the reward structure has and should have more to do with performance than abstract ideals about the worth of disciplines. The first case study in this chapter reflects both the general resistance to change and the special interest shown in questions dealing with variability in faculty compensation.

CASE STUDY

Sally Saddlemire is in the midst of her first year as academic dean at Swansdowne College. She came to her position after ten years on the faculty of a rather prestigious liberal arts college and is concerned that dedication and commitment at Swansdowne are less than she thinks they need to be. Unlike her former institution, the environment at Swansdowne is that of a middle-rank college with a rather traditional, middle-aged faculty of somewhat mixed credentials and accomplishments.

There had been little faculty hiring in recent years. In fact, there was a difficult period five years ago after an unexpected dip in student enrollment when several faculty, including two tenured professors, had to be released. Salaries have been low for some time and there is little prospect of substantial increases. Not surprisingly, faculty morale is not very high.

Sally feels strongly that any extra resources the college acquires should be used to reward the relatively few faculty who appear to be performing at a consistently high level. Because of the restricted budgetary situation, however, the college has fallen into a pattern of across-the-board percentage salary increases, with the senior faculty leadership insisting that trying to make merit determinations is not "worth the trouble." Unfortunately, some of the senior faculty are among those who seem to have slackened off.

Just the other day, one of the bright younger faculty members had complained to Sally that the system was stacked against him and that the institution was not rewarding effort and accomplishment. Sally knows that another younger professor has scheduled an appointment this afternoon, and she anticipates a similar complaint. She would like to be encouraging and reassuring to these productive faculty members. She knows, however, that the feelings against merit pay run rather strongly through the senior faculty leadership. She doesn't want to precipitate a cause célèbre in her first year as dean.

What advice—both short-term and long-term—would you give to Sally?

Response # 1

Dean Saddlemire has inherited a flock of faculty dinosaurs, along with a budget that is nearly as dry as the Gobi. She must break the continued pattern of the across-the-board syndrome and create a new environment that will permit, in the long term, a performance-based evaluation system. In the short term, Dean Saddlemire must put her limited incremental salary resources into a rewards program recognizing the younger faculty's research efforts and defusing the senior faculty's opposition by teaching excellence awards. The "bonus" nature of these awards must meet three tests to be credible: (1) They must be limited to truly outstanding individuals only; (2) be of a sufficiently large dollar amount; and (3) be annualized into succeeding year's salaries.

In the lead time thus achieved, Dean Saddlemire can put an ad hoc faculty task force together with some balance between the dinosaurs and the Young Turks. The task force will be assigned the goals of achieving a thorough study of current performance evaluation research. Saddlemire should save a few of her "eggs" to retain a nationally recognized consultant to assist the task force as an honest broker. The consultant can save hours of committee time and add the impetus of the outside expert to the proceedings. Senior faculty at Swansdowne College are archetypical in their negative feelings about "merit pay." Time will be required to overcome their resistance and their ingrained adverse attitudes and long-held convictions toward the terminology. These negatives are difficult to uproot and replace by a positive performance-evaluation system that rewards both teaching and research with an even hand.

Hopefully, this proposed plan of action will allow both Dean Saddlemire and her faculty dinosaurs to survive the Ice Age of scarce financial resources. (O. E. Lovell, Vice President for Academic Affairs, Nicholls State University, Thibodaux, Louisiana.)

Response # 2

In her first year, Sally Saddlemire has found herself in the now classic wintering position of the North American *Deanus academus.* This season finds deans crouched strategically behind their desks, balancing the fiscal realities of their institutions with their professional creativity and personal charm, tools constantly in a state of deterioration. Remarkable to any who have lived through Dean Saddlemire's first year is that in such a posture, once the "possible" is ruled out, the apparently "impossible" begins to look pretty good.

Take, for example, the simple and most obvious problem facing Sally. Her faculty are underpaid and she doesn't have the funds to begin changing the situation. Many deans have faced that very moment with the same initial reaction: "Well, if I don't have it, what can I do?" Thus the retreat into the simplicity and comfort of across-the-board salary increases.

Oddly enough, much of the answer to the problem of limited compensation isn't to be found in the area of finances at all. Finances didn't bring most of us to the university and finances alone will probably not drive us away. We continue to prize highly our flexible schedules, both daily and seasonal; working conditions that are some of the most humane of any industry; and the opportunities for collegial support and stimulating social relations that make the academic life a delightful career prospect. It is to these dimensions of Swansdowne College that Sally must attend. For though her efforts will not substitute for the institution's obligation to provide a just wage, they will help to keep the issue in perspective.

It is in such situations, most of all, that the human art of deaning is called upon. While applying steady and appropriate pressure on the salary structure, Sally must ask herself, "What am I doing to improve the overall quality of life for my faculty and college?" Recognizing that the intensity of concern about low salaries is inversely proportional to how well faculty feel they are being supported and respected in the other aspects of their professional life, Sally must train her creative attention on those areas where her influence may be greater. After all, she does have much to say regarding the most creative and faculty-affirming use of course scheduling throughout the year; one can presume that she does manage some resources, limited as they may be, for faculty travel and development; oftentimes Sally must make decisions regarding the allocation or reallocation of support equipment—for example, personal computers. And close to the top of the list is Sally's influence in creating occasions for professional and personal "satisfaction opportunities." We all must feel that our abilities and judgments are appreciated and respected. Sally's careful and *personal* hand in matching faculty with exciting courses and program opportunities can go a long way with faculty who seek a diversity of rewards.

Sally, however, has already had one visitor and another is on the way. Such visits have existential import and thus require rather existential solutions. My advice: Dean Saddlemire, don't avoid this one, especially in your inaugural year. You are being asked, and rightly so, "What's your position on retaining and encouraging high quality in the faculty?" Out of answers to such questions are deans lost and found. Your response will have long-term consequences for both your deanship and your college. But you are wise to not go head to head with your senior faculty leadership too soon—if ever. Take advantage of the interest your young faculty have shown in the issue. Ask them and several carefully selected respected faculty (who you believe would appreciate your perspective on encouraging quality effort and accomplishment) to take this issue up and make recommendations to you and the faculty. This avoids the dangers of a dean's mandate as well as providing young faculty with a productive avenue to the examination of a serious issue. Your Solomon-like decision allows you to maintain your professional integrity, respect the history of the college and, indeed, provide just another non-financial argument on behalf of Swansdowne College—namely, a sensitive and professionally competent academic dean. (G. David Pollick, Dean of Arts and Sciences, Seattle University, Seattle, Washington.)

Both responses make it clear that this is a subject to be treated persistently but slowly. The first response (Vice President Lovell) reminds us of the value of time-gaining strategies. During the time gained, the energies of the faculty can be harnessed toward the end of determining if a shift in policy is desirable. The second response (Dean Pollick) reminds us that there are rewards other than salary that a dean can work with to support productivity. Implicit in both responses is the notion that the question should be pushed back into the faculty. An important part of effective deaning is to know when a question is answerable and when it requires more time and work. Some deans may seek to provide answers too quickly, only to discover that the answers provided, while eminently sensible, are really acceptable only to themselves.

Faculty will often push a dean or provost for an answer. They can recognize weaseling a mile away and generally don't like it. If they can get an answer, they then have something (and someone) to attack. This is a lot easier for them than confronting the ambiguities, conflicts, and value judgments involved in making an answer work. An effective dean or provost will find the line between answering too quickly that which cannot be well answered and weaseling. As the faculty learn that their dean or provost can find that line, they will be less tempted to trap him or her into overly simplistic responses to very difficult issues. It is also clear that no matter how it is approached, merit pay will continue to be among those difficult issues.

Faculty Entrepreneurship

The definitions of consulting are murky on many campuses. Furthermore, questions dealing with the appropriateness of various kinds of consulting activities and the matter of "how much is too much?" seem to be in the air in many departments. Entrepreneurial activity can pose a severe challenge and threat to institutional collegiality when consulting activities are much more frequent in a few departments than elsewhere in the institution. Traditional understandings of appropriate responsibilities can be easily upset and the balance between teaching, research, and public service skewed. Since financial rewards are clearly at stake, emotions surrounding issues of fairness and justice can be quickly engaged. Other values may also be involved, for part of the ethic of inquiry and of assessment requires dispassionate and objective judgments that may become difficult once the likelihood of personal rewards is introduced. Certainly, community difficulties can also occur, as the following case study illustrates.

CASE STUDY

Provost Template had no difficulty understanding the value of consulting. After all, as a young geologist he had regularly supplemented his salary that way in years now long past. Overall, entrepreneurship was fine, Template felt. He did wish, however, that there were easier ways to sort out some of the conflicting values it seemed to involve. For instance, right now he could think of four faculty, including one department chair, who were rumored to be selling real estate on the side, even though real estate had little to do with their disciplines. None was overtly abusing the institutional relationship, so far as he knew, but neither was the institutional good being advanced. Furthermore, he could not very well dictate how faculty chose to spend time outside the institution without stirring up a real hornet's nest. Still, he was beginning to feel uneasy about the image the institution might be developing in the local community as a result of some of the consulting and other entrepreneurial activities of the faculty.

Image was becoming a problem in connection with an otherwise excellent department of electrical engineering. Template had already gotten several barbed comments at the Rotary Club from owners of two area engineering consulting firms. The gist of their complaints was that the engineering faculty were presenting unfair competition in their consulting activities by selling their services too cheaply. It was pointed out that none of the faculty had the overhead expenses of the firms. It did not seem fair, his Rotary friends pointed out, that the very public that paid taxes to support the state institution should be placed at a competitive disadvantage by that institution's employees.

As provost, Template had talked with the dean of engineering several times about the matter, but had not gotten very far. The bulk of the dean's responses had focused on the values to the institution of consulting and the adequacy of the new policies on patents and copyrights. He had added that he was reluctant to intrude on the academic freedom of the professors. When pressed on the image problem, the dean quietly pointed out that he thought the local engineering consulting firms were price gougers and clearly overcharging for what they provided. Besides, he continued, most of them couldn't offer the diversity, expertise, and experience that his faculty could.

At any rate, the dean concluded, although salaries in electrical engineering at the university were several thousand dollars ahead, on the average, of salaries in nonengineering departments, they were still way below market. He made it rather clear to Template that unless the institution could provide an increase of $5,000 to $10,000 per engineering faculty member, his people would have to continue to supplement their incomes or he was going to lose them to more lucrative industry offers. Provost Template, for his part, knew that such an increase was impossible. For one thing, he didn't have the money. Beyond that, the liberal arts faculty were beginning to become ugly in their comments about the overpaid philistines who had invaded the faculty. Still, he expected the public relations problems to worsen and spill over to trustees and legislators unless he did something to tighten up further the university's policies on consulting. The problem was that he really didn't have a clue as to what might help the situation.

What options does Provost Template have and which one(s) would you advise him to pursue?

Response # 1

Provost Template faces a problem that is very much alive on many campuses today. Aside from the "hard" issue of consulting by faculty members, he seems to confront, at least in his own mind, the "soft" issue of the image of the university. He probably does believe that an ounce of image is worth a pound of performance.

From the evidence presented, it seems that the university lacks a clear policy on such matters as time allowed to faculty members for consulting, consulting pay received by faculty members, and consulting as research or service. Further, it seems clear that little, if any, dialogue has taken place between university officials and local practitioners, thus allowing a setting in which some of the Rotary Club "wheels" can utter their barbed comments. In this litigious age, the off-campus consulting firms might well consider some class-action suit—"do unto others . . ."—in the manner of physicians who have brought suit against universities that operate health service units.

What options are available to Provost Template? Terminating the dean, terminating engineering, or replacing earned consulting fees with university "hard money" all seem untenable solutions and would result in barbed comments from other constituents. What is needed are some positive solutions.

Here are some positive solutions that might be brought to bear on this situation:

1. Writing or rewriting university policies and procedures on consulting, specifying how much time faculty members can devote to it, disposition of fees earned, approvals needed, when consulting is considered research, service, or private business, and monitoring of consulting efforts and time to make sure that the university and the engineering students are not being short-changed by entrepreneurial professors.

2. Provost Template and the dean of engineering could begin to redirect the energies and imaginations of the faculty members into research programs funded by off-campus agencies and non-

profit organizations. If this were done, the professors, the university, and the students would all benefit, and unfair competition with local firms would cease.

3. To promote better cooperation among on-campus and off-campus professionals, the university and city officials could establish a new research-development-technology park, in which federal, state, university, and private dollars would work together for improved economic growth of the area, state, and region.

4. The dean of engineering could set up an advisory body of professional engineers to meet regularly with him and the engineering faculty. While the main purpose of the advisory body would be to assist the engineering college, much goodwill and understanding could accrue from such meetings and cooperative ventures.

5. At a higher level, the university president and provost should meet regularly with city officials to anticipate problems such as this one and take some preventative action, if that were called for.

6. Provost Template should meet with the liberal arts faculty regularly, to sprinkle on them some "tender loving care," and remind them that without engineering there would be fewer students and, quite possibly, fewer faculty positions. He should also assist them in seeking research funds for some of their scholarly or service work.

The elements seem right for the provost to seize an opportunity right at his doorstep. In taking the initiative and implementing these six options, his own image and that of the university would be positively enhanced in the community and in the legislature. The best advice to Provost Template: *Carpe diem!* (Robert E. Wolverton, formerly Vice President for Academic Affairs, Mississippi State University, Mississippi State, Mississippi.)

Response # 2

Provost Template's recognition that he needs to further tighten up the university's policies on consulting is a pretty good place to begin. Faculty need to know what is expected of them; and the greater community that supports the university is entitled to consider the principles and academic rationale that guides the institution. Although people of good will will continue to disagree, clear and well-articulated thinking would certainly lessen tension and give trustees, legislators, and university administrators more readily defendable positions.

In developing such a policy, Provost Template would be well advised to consider the role that consulting plays in the *academic* life of the university. In so doing, the rather sticky issue of personal time versus professional time would no doubt surface. Although the problem is probably not as complex in the university as it is in industry, the distinction is by no means cut and dried. Whether or not Template's institution approves of such nonacademic activities as selling real estate, it needs to be up front on the issue, with appropriate guidelines laid out in the faculty handbook. Nonacademic activities then become resolved on the basis of the faculty person's contractual obligations. However, let not the simplicity of the solution be misleading. More than one administrator has lost his or her grip on this world before having a new or revised handbook approved.

The issue of image comes more to the academic point. Provost Template's rationale on behalf of consulting must be first and last an academic rationale. Though it can be gently indicated that the university salary structure is simply not competitive in the market of such fields as electrical engineering, even if it were there would be good educational reasons for the faculty's involvement in their respective professional fields outside the university. To allow the issue of salary to be the focus of the discussion is to deprecate the real and most important values involved in faculty consultation. The Rotary would hardly be the place for Template to defend his faculty's actions on financial grounds.

The provost can certainly turn to the dean of engineering for a clear and precise—and since he's a dean, no doubt eloquent—statement of the necessity for professional faculty to remain rooted in the state-of-the-art activities of their fields. One can be sure that the public who support the university expect its graduates in electrical engineering to be as current in their knowledge as possible. In many fields it's a case of public safety. No doubt the community's engineering firms must recognize this as well—at least their professional associations do. This is usually the case with the accrediting bodies of most professional schools as well. The quality of a professional faculty is commonly recognized as closely aligned with the depth and quality of participation in its fields at large. Certainly, the quality of a faculty is an academic issue.

My advice to Provost Template: Wheel out your biggest guns.
You're in the business of educational excellence. Barriers placed
in the way of providing the highest quality faculty prevent you
fulfilling the responsibility the university has to the greater tax-
paying public: students, parents, and the larger community that
will depend upon your young professionals. Say all this well,
Provost, and say it in writing. (G. David Pollick, Dean of Arts
and Sciences, Seattle University, Seattle, Washington.)

Response # 3

Although both of the situations that Provost Template faces involve
entrepreneurship and consulting, the problems are different
enough to demand different approaches. The case study uses the
terms "entrepreneurship" and "consulting" almost interchange-
ably, which, in an ideal academic world, they are. However, in
the first example—that of faculty selling real estate—the entrepreneurial activity cannot be classified as consulting because it
has little relationship to the faculty members' academic disciplines.
When outside consulting by faculty is related to scholarly work,
it benefits the faculty themselves as well as the university, outside
clients, and often the public at large. It is an effective way to
disseminate the findings of academic research, it enables the faculty members to interact with private-sector scientists and scholars
in the same field, and it helps to narrow the gap between academic
and industrial salaries.

Selling real estate, on the other hand, offers none of these
benefits, but instead poses a number of potential hazards. When
faculty work below their professional stature, they demean rather
than enhance their own reputations and that of the institution.
They diminish to some degree the educational, professional, and
personal development of both their students and themselves. Although the case study does not refer overtly to abuse of time,
faculty members who are selling real estate are diverting time
and intellectual resources away from creative and scientific
thought related to their academic work. In contrast, those who
are consulting in their own fields are augmenting the work they
do during the traditional workday.

The tenure system precludes using threats of termination to
punish faculty members engaging in undesirable activities. Even
if it did not, however, a more positive approach would be for

Provost Template to encourage faculty members involved to channel their entrepreneurial efforts in a more appropriate direction. He should advocate their doing consulting work related to their academic disciplines and point out that the long-term financial payoffs of such efforts will probably equal or even exceed those derived from selling real estate. He should also make them aware that consulting will further their academic careers, which in theory should be their highest priority. Publications might result from such work, or it might lead to future collaborative research projects with private-sector scientists—results that are certainly not possible if they use their free time to sell real estate.

The institution could also make some minor but compelling policy changes to encourage appropriate consulting. Promotion criteria could be extended to include consideration of consulting work if it leads to demonstrable benefits for the faculty, their students, or the university. The institution could also help faculty identify consulting opportunities by maintaining and advertising a computerized database of campus expertise. Finally, the university should not only censure those who disregard institutional policies, but also publicly praise those whose efforts are more consistent with academic goals.

The case of the electrical engineering consultants is more difficult because no one has committed any real wrongdoing. The advantages of faculty consulting outlined here obviously apply to these individuals: They are consulting in their field, a perfectly legitimate use of their free time and one with the potential to benefit all involved parties in terms of enhancing the educational mission of the university. It is true that universities should not provide services at below-market fees, thereby presenting unfair competition to private businesses. Nor should they provide—at any price—services readily available from commercial sources.

On the other hand, the arguments against allowing the faculty to charge allegedly low fees draw attention to the fundamental differences between the academic and private sectors—differences that should be fostered rather than obliterated. If faculty consulting fees actually are lower than those changed by private consultants, that is because an individual not encumbered by the expenses of a business can afford to provide services for less. It is not clear, however, that substantial differences do exist between private and academic consulting fees. To resolve the issue with facts rather than perceptions, Provost Template might consider commissioning a study to compare consulting fees. If the data indicate that the gap is as wide as it is perceived to be, faculty should not be averse to a suggestion that they raise their fees slightly to make them more consistent with those charged by consultants working in private firms.

Thus the provost's main line of defense must be to educate the public rather than to change the behavior of his faculty; their right to consult should be upheld, not undermined. The provost needs to convince the private firms that the faculty consultants are providing a service that they are not providing or cannot provide; that is, that the academic engineers have skills or information not available to the private-sector consultants. This should counter their claim that the university is presenting unfair competition.

Taken separately, these two examples illustrate well both the hazards and the advantages of outside consulting by faculty. Taken together, they demonstrate the impossibility of using one rigid set of rules to deal with all outside faculty activities. It instantly becomes obvious that such issues must be considered on a case-by-case basis and that decisions should always be based on how well the activities mesh with institutional goals and policies. (L. Leon Campbell, Provost, University of Deleware, Newark, Deleware.)

As the responses indicate, there are several aspects to dealing effectively with the consulting/entrepreneurship component of academic life. The first response (Former Vice President Wolverton) describes a variety of initiatives that could be taken to ameliorate the situation. The second response (Dean Pollick) focuses on relating consulting and entrepreneurial activities to the academic life of the university. Where these matters are clarified and made policy through faculty debate and, ultimately, handbook revision, everyone can have a better sense of when his or her activities are helpful to the realization of the goals, priorities, and missions of the institution, when they might be harmful, and when they are simply irrelevant. In all of this, Dean Pollick argues, the ultimate rationales must be academic in nature. The third response (Provost Campbell) is based on the recognition that consulting and entrepreneurial activities may be quite different things. The response deals with a number of practical matters relating to each, and offers suggestions on how to deal with them, including advice on the need to educate public figures as well as university personnel about the appropriate role of consulting and entrepreneurial activities in academic life.

The Picket Line

Collective bargaining is no stranger to the college campus. Many institutions have had negotiated agreements with support staff and/ or faculty for some time. Although the pace at which additional institutions are taking up collective bargaining has slowed considerably, it still enjoys an upward trend.

Experience makes a great difference in how the negotiation process and surrounding relationships are handled. There is often a maturation process, which leads to clearer understandings and shared expectations within both the bargaining unit and management after they have gone through several cycles of contract negotiations and implementation. By contrast, institutions experiencing unionization or a strike for the first time face a variety of new issues and decisions, as the following case study illustrates.

CASE STUDY

Before breakfast, Joe had already read the full-page advertisement in the metropolitan newspaper. At first he wondered who could have afforded it, but such mild curiosity faded as he looked more closely at the text. All of the students and faculty were being urged to boycott the campus and not to cross the picket lines set up to protest the institution's refusal to meet the demands of the new clerical staff union.

As vice president for academic affairs and provost, Joe was not surprised to see some of the names of those who had signed the advertisement, though he was startled to see that they had listed their departmental affiliations and rank. Several were approaching tenure or promotion decisions later in the year, Joe knew, and he could just see the difficulties that would arise if any of the decisions were negative. The faculty union would surely claim that the "real" reason behind any negative decision was resentment of the professor's courage and public dedication to principle.

That, however, was a future problem, and more immediate ones were at hand. Phone calls from faculty had started to come in even before he reached his office. Some proposed that they conduct classes at home and were calling to secure Joe's blessing. Others were announcing their commitment to the status quo, and one or two had already demanded that any professor who failed to meet classes on campus should be docked pay. The call from one of the laboratory instructors was particularly poignant, as she felt committed both to better pay for the clerical staff and to providing the students the instruction they were paying for—instruction that could not adequately be provided outside the campus laboratory setting.

Fortunately, Joe was not a member of the administration team bargaining with the clerical union. The institution decided some years ago, wisely Joe thought, that the provost could be either the premier implementor of contracts or involved in negotiating them, not both.

Joe knew that most faculty and students shared his belief in the importance of the work they do together, and hence would be on the job. Joe also knew that over-reaction on his part could further escalate the difficulty.

What options does Joe have and which one(s) would you advise him to pursue?

Response # 1

Joe may not know it yet, but he has very few options if he wishes to remain credible with the administration and board members responsible for employee relations at the university. Spokesperson and advocate for faculty he may be, but in the messiness of a strike he will not win, and there is no popular line for a negotiator to take.

Because the handling of this clerical strike creates precedents for the university that may reach to the faculty union, the boiler engineers, the health service nurses, and the custodial and food service employees, Joe must be absolutely sure of the implications of his utterances. His placating "yes" to paying the laboratory instructor for meeting her classes at home denies the negotiating officers chips they will need when final settlement is approaching. His yes to Ms. Laboratory becomes a precedent years down the road for clerical workers who do not wish to cross the faculty's picket lines. That same yes on Joe's campus may haunt another public agency in the state faced with an employee strike, albeit on very different issues.

And so, Management Joe, your political pronoun is "we." Your bargaining units are "they." Remember that the strike requires your team to organize a public relations office, generate a steady stream of public announcements of victories, and to cackle over the clerical union's inability to orchestrate a decent strike. Never mind if management is faltering, the union triumphing; the Rhetoric of Bull is essential political nonsense. Give the dirty work to your public information officer and keep yourself and the others out of it.

First off, Joe, make it clear. Classes must meet at the hours and at the sites described in the registration schedule. Refer to that document as a contract. If classes are not held at that time and place, salary may be docked pro-rata.

That, Joe, means you who wanted to be provost in order to facilitate discussion of Great Ideas, are now to organize a corps of inspectors—your fellow administrators, whatever their titles— to stalk the campus with clipboards every hour on the hour to check that classes are held. Good luck persuading your late 1960s activist-turned-assistant provost that this is her job.

Of course, Joe, you need to beware of over-reaction, of escalation. But by talking tough on pay you've got some ground on which you can be more flexible. Keep in mind, too, that the initial disbelief of many liberals in the faculty that striking or refusing to cross a picket line means loss of income can be tempered by your reminding them that the real labor heroes would have viewed the taking of wages as wrong (cite John L. Lewis, James Petrillo, The Wobblies, whomever, but outcite the union's advocates).

Cynicism aside, you need to keep communication developing with the clerical union on wages, hours, and working conditions. You need to demonstrate that your differences with your valued secretaries are professional, not personal. You need to counsel all people that the strike will eventually end, that people must live together in respect. Remind them of the poison that develops if old friends, neighbors, and colleagues cut one another dead at the supermarket and the wedding reception. Again, remind folks of the ability of the UAW and GM bosses to have a drink together at the end of some pretty acrimonious negotiating. That may be an apocryphal drink, but it's worth toasting.

The high road thus taken, it's time for hardball again. If you won't play, Joe, someone tougher will—and you'll be reading the last pages of *The Chronicle*. You have to answer immediate questions from students, parents, reporters—"If those labs aren't held as scheduled, will students get their credits?" That's the bottom line for most folks, the issue that could make or break the strike. And that means that you say "Probably not. The university's concern for academic quality requires of each professor, etc., etc., etc."

When that bomb hits the student union, prepare for another attack. The press will ask about scabs. Be clear that the university may begin advertising for part-time and other adjunct faculty. Emeriti, desperate "position sought" advertisers, and your fellow administrators are fair game. Remind the press that faculty who give up teaching give up their normal managerial influence in hiring and curriculum.

Conclude Joe, back on principles. Speak of the right of students to learn and teachers to teach. And remember, other administrators on your negotiating team are able to handle some of the heavy lines I've written into your script. Remember, too, balance your tough line with a compassionate face when you meet those clerical employees.

Postscript: There are some intriguing issues in this strike. Are faculty walkouts legal or could they be termed secondary boycotts? Perhaps the university should seek an injunction from the courts on the faculty issue—thus, among other things, muddying the waters for the clerical union. (David Johnson, Dean of the College, Gustavus Adolphus College, St. Peter, Minnesota.)

Response # 2

Joe is in a bind. As provost of an institution of higher learning he has a contractual obligation to ensure that students are not denied the education the university has promised them, but he also needs to make his and the university's commitment to collegiality and social justice exceedingly clear.

Joe's goals must be to settle the strike quickly and to heal the wound the strike has already caused. His challenge is to stake out the moral high ground in the situation. But, he must also act quickly and decisively.

Joe has the following options: (1) advise faculty and students to respect the picket lines and cancel all classes until the strike is settled; (2) advise faculty and students to respect the picket lines and arrange for off-campus classes until the strike is settled; (3) advise faculty and students to cross the picket lines; (4) advise faculty and students to consult their consciences and decide on their own whether or not to cross the picket lines; and (5) issue no statement.

Joe can not realistically exercise options 4 or 5. Taking no action or advising faculty to make individual decisions would resolve the ambiguity of the moment, but either recommendation would be viewed as indecision and thus would weaken his position with all parties. Similarly, Joe cannot really advise faculty to arrange for off-campus teaching. Not only would this action cause logistical confusion, but it would also almost certainly violate the terms of the university's liability insurance.

So, Joe must decide to advise faculty either to cross or not to cross the picket lines. After consulting with the university counsel and gaining the support of his president, Joe should issue a statement informing faculty and students that classes will meet as scheduled. Joe's statement should also direct faculty, department heads, and university administrators to staff their offices with appropriate supervisory personnel.

Joe must recognize, however, that strikes polarize people and that in critical situations people want to feel they can have influence on the outcome. Accordingly, he should announce that there will be an open forum that afternoon and that classes will be cancelled for two hours to enable everyone to attend. This forum will allow people to air their views—vent, if necessary—and enable those who are so inclined to show their support for the union. It will also communicate to the union and its supporters that the university has regard for them, recognizes the seriousness of the situation, and is willing to listen.

Joe must also issue assurances to faculty who decide to respect the picket lines that the university recognizes their right of free speech and affirms their right to support the union. He should, however, stop short of stating that there will be no recriminations because such a statement might be viewed as a veiled threat. Joe needs to draw upon the trust he has established over the years

and he must, in days to come, frequently restate his readiness
to help resolve the dilemma.

The clerical staff union and faculty and students who support
the strike will not be pleased with Joe's statement. The best Joe
can hope for is that his actions will encourage these groups to
keep open the lines of communication with the administration.
The faculty and students who do not support the strike and the
trustees almost certainly will recognize the wisdom of Joe's efforts
to keep the dialogue going and to rebuild trust in the university
community.

In addition, Joe needs to put intense pressure on the bargaining teams to settle the strike quickly. His announcement
should indicate that he is recommending to the administration
and the union that they engage in nonstop bargaining until the
strike is settled. He should also communicate in private to the
chief negotiators that he thinks it would be in the interests of all
parties if each bargaining team reconsidered its position. In short,
Joe needs to use force *and* moral suasion to move the negotiators
off dead-center.

Finally, Joe needs to specify that since classes will be held as
scheduled, students will be obliged to fulfill course requirements
for sessions they miss if they support the strike. However, he
should also urge faculty to be flexible about arranging for makeup
work.

The strike is already a reality. Joe needs to work to avoid its
prolongment. Strikes are critical moments in the history of organizations, and this strike can bitterly affect the university for
years to come if it is not settled quickly and in a manner that
enables all parties to rededicate themselves to the primary mission
of the institution. Joe's strategy of keeping everyone focused on
this higher goal should prove useful. (Robert W. Gordon, Associate Provost, Siena Heights College, Adrian, Michigan.)

Both respondentents make it clear that classes must go on.
The first response (Dean Johnson) recognizes the inevitable "we"
and "they" of the bargaining situation and urges "Management
Joe" to get on with it. He describes some of the other steps the
administration will have to take as the bargaining continues. The
second response (Associate Provost Gordon) lays out the options
and argues that deliberate steps must be taken to bring about an
early settlement.

The union may want an early settlement—and it may not. Sometimes organizing efforts on other campuses or even in other states require that the union hang tough regardless of the local issues on any particular campus experiencing a strike. Where this is the case, even additional concessions by the university is unlikely to end the strike. These things are rarely neat.

In this situation the chief academic officer may have to live with the consequences of his or her actions for a long time. Continuing awareness of this certainty can help him or her to leave unsaid negative observations about the behavior of others. However accurate these might be, they will not ultimately contribute to the common cause.

Program Duplication and the State Coordinating Office

State coordinating offices, state commissions on higher education, and, in some cases, fully staffed state departments of higher education have become increasingly important in recent years. These bodies, created by state legislators, represent the public's interest in gaining control commensurate with the public cost of higher education. They also represent the state's interests in keeping the federal government from becoming further involved in regulating higher education.

There are two issues that state agencies find their way to sooner or later. The first is equity in funding. The realization that one institution is being funded more richly than another for comparable work has lead to complex definitions of comparable work and elaborate formulas for translating various parameters—for example, credit hours completed—into dollars allocated.

The second issue likely to emerge is that of program duplication. On the surface it seems wasteful to the taxpayer and the legislator that similar or identical programs exist in neighboring institutions. There is likely to be periodic pressure to trim one or the other and thereby reduce the costs to the state. Arguments about balance within an institution can be offset by arguments about balance within the state. Whether or not a state needs, for instance, four law schools becomes a question likely to be brought into state coordinating bodies. That there are no empirical answers to such questions again spins out a variety of ways of looking at, measuring, and trying to do something about program duplication.

While the primary concern of state coordinating bodies continues to be the public colleges and universities in the state, private institutions are not immune from the effects of their consideration. As private institutions increasingly approach state bodies for financial support—for instance, for creating a barrier-free campus in compliance with state and/or federal law—they become more vulnerable to the standards those bodies use for dealing with such questions whether they arise in the public or the private sector. Furthermore, in curricular matters the consequences can become quite severe. If a state decides it doesn't have enough programs of a certain type—for example, nursing—and that it will accordingly "fund up" the state institutions to develop them, the consequences for similar programs in private institutions can lead to a serious competitive disadvantage for these institutions.

In any case, state coordinating bodies appear to be here to stay. University and college administrators, particularly deans and provosts, are becoming increasingly caught up in issues that transcend their campus, as the following case study shows.

CASE STUDY

Dean Wilson reflected that Urbane State College had done well with the new interior design program. It had been started just in the nick of time five years ago when the enrollments in the criminal justice and urban recreation programs had started to plunge. Looking back at that time, Wilson wondered how he would have been able to keep these two programs without the additional credit hours that interior design had generated. Even with them, Wilson had been forced to lay off several faculty members in urban recreation and one in criminal justice. Things had been quite difficult, but were now finally looking better.

All of this reflection had been provoked by Wilson's reading the letter his president had forwarded to him from the State Commission for Higher Education. The newly arrived commissioner had announced his determination to eliminate program duplication among the state regional campuses, and the commission had enthusiastically endorsed it. He was apparently starting his campaign without delay, for the letter notified Urbane that the interior design program appeared to duplicate unnecessarily a similar program at Upstate Tech. The commissioner also noted that the other program was both older and served more students. The letter concluded with the announcement that a special panel had been appointed to review the interior design programs and that Urbane officials should be prepared to appear before it to justify the program at their college. The president would appear, of course, but Wilson knew that his would have to be the major voice in the proceedings.

Looking at the names of those on the panel provided Wilson no comfort. The names he recognized were those of people he suspected of favoring interests in the northern part of the state. To be sure, they were in the minority on the list, but Wilson had no idea about the sympathies of the others. So far as the number of students in the interior design program was concerned, Upstate may have more, but Wilson felt confident that his college had better. He was not clear about the credentials of the faculty at Upstate, but the faculty at Urbane were solid folks and the program was enriched by the part-time practitioners they had been able to enlist. All this made him feel reasonably good at first blush, but he was troubled about how to proceed.

Specifically, he wondered how to approach the interior design business community in obtaining support for the Urbane program and what tack to take with the state commission. He knew he could count on the support of two local legislators, but didn't know how best to use them. Most pressing at the moment were the student reporters who had gotten wind of the panel and who wanted to know whether there would continue to be an interior design program or whether students should start making plans to transfer. If the students were alarmed, he knew the faculty members would be not far behind.

How would you advise Wilson to proceed?

Response # 1

It is often said that the best defense is a well-planned offense. Before Dean Wilson embarks on a campaign, he needs to gather evidence about the interior design program. For in the end his most powerful arguments for program continuation before the State Commission for Higher Education will rest on qualitative matters. If he has strong supporting evidence, then Dean Wilson's most telling thrusts will center on the program's excellence and its usefulness to the region and state.

The dean should assemble data about the quality of students who have entered and graduated from the interior design program. Placement data are particularly relevant; assuming that this is an upper division program, at least three years of placement data should be available. Anecdotal information about the program's quality should be gathered from graduates; anecdotal information about graduates' effectiveness should be gathered from employers.

Market survey information regarding employability of interior design graduates—based on local, regional, state, and national projections—should be developed. The national accrediting agency for interior design programs should be able to provide some such information. Local and state interior design business leaders could supply useful employment information regarding present conditions and future potentials.

Faculty are at the heart of the instructional program. The dean should have faculty profiles developed, study them himself, then subject them to scrutiny by someone in the field of interior design upon whose judgment he can rely. The dean needs to know more about his faculty than that they are solid folks. Similar scrutiny should be given to the program of study offered to students. Instructional resources such as library, dedicated equipment, and design collections should be assessed. A consultant suggested by the national accrediting agency could give the dean a useful analysis with respect to faculty, program, and resources.

Assuming that the foregoing information and analyses are supportive of the interior design program and the market for its graduates, the dean should consider the following, after clearance by the provost and president:

1. Prepare a one- or two-page brief that describes the program's benefits to students and the state, emphasizes the program's excellence in terms of content, students, and faculty, and makes the point for "necessary duplication." Quotes from interior design business leaders and the national accrediting association would be useful.

2. Circulate this up-beat brief among students, reporters, and the press-at-large. Get student support.

3. Circulate the brief among concerned state commission staff as well as the commissioners.

4. Arrange for commission staff to visit the campus and program and to meet informally with students, graduates, faculty, and supportive business people. The visit should be arranged so that it is positive and nonconfrontational. Stay in the background and let students, grads, faculty, and business people do his talking.

5. Be sure that the special panel's staff is well briefed on his program's strengths; if possible, arrange for program students and graduates to testify before the panel. Testimony from business leaders will be useful. Make sure that his own presentation is positive; avoid comparisons between his program's qualities and those of Upstate. Make the case for necessary duplication or make the case that his program is different.

6. Generally, it's best not to invite legislators to pressure such a commission and especially its staff. The staff will be around and will resent that pressure long after the politicians are gone.

Throughout the review process it is important for the dean to maintain positive, cooperative relationships with the commission, the special panel, and the staff of those two agencies. Among students and faculty, Dean Wilson should project the view that program review by appropriate external agencies is to be expected and that Urbane State College has an opportunity here to show its excellence. (Paul Ford, Vice President for Academic Affairs, Western Washington University, Bellingham, Washington.)

Response # 2

The circumstance encountered by Dean Wilson is complex but not unusual in public higher education. There are a number of constituencies Dean Wilson must take into consideration in contemplating the best strategy for success in his endeavor to retain the new interior design program. The following commentary indicates an approach that might be taken with each individual or group.

President

Assuming that Dean Wilson reports to the president and the president favors retaining the program, Dean Wilson should schedule a meeting with the president and propose a well-considered strategy for attempting to retain the program. The strategy should include the steps outlined next and take a proactive approach to the problem so that the president has a number of options to consider in preparation for the meeting with the special panel and commission.

Department Chair and Program Faculty

After the president and dean have agreed on the approach to be taken, the dean should meet with the department chair and, perhaps, program faculty. The dean should indicate that the college will attempt to retain the program. Suggestions should be sought regarding the identification of a respected consultant who can be hired to examine the program and prepare a report that addresses the quality and uniqueness of the program and how it can be differentiated from the one at Upstate Tech. The report also should focus on those aspects of the Urbane State College program that might make it vulnerable to a negative recommendation from the panel and commissioner and how those potential weaknesses can be addressed.

Current Students and Alumni of the Program

Students currently enrolled in the program, as well as alumni of the program, should be informed that the college is seeking to retain the program. The students should be told that even if their efforts are unsuccessful, those currently enrolled in the program will be allowed to complete their studies before the program is terminated. This is standard practice. If alumni have not been surveyed recently, they should be polled to ascertain their perception of the strengths and weaknesses of the program so that the strengths can be used in the presentation to the panel and the weaknesses addressed internally. Both students and alumni should be encouraged to write letters of support for the retention of the program to Dean Wilson for later use in making a case for the program.

Business Community

Two facets of the business community should be addressed: the interior design business people and the local chamber of commerce. Each group should be acquainted with the problems faced by the program, and support should be solicited from each constituency. The interior design business people should be asked to write letters to Dean Wilson attesting to the quality of the program and the extent to which students in or graduates of the program have been helpful to their businesses. The chamber of commerce should be asked to write a letter of support for the program commenting on the positive impact of the program—including its faculty and students—on the business climate in the community.

Local Legislators

The two local legislators should be made aware of the letter from the commissioner and informed of the strategy the college plans to follow. They should be asked about the type of help they might be willing to provide. Assuming a good relationship exists between the institutional leadership and the legislators, a scenario should be agreed upon and followed. The most likely assistance the local legislators could provide initially would be a letter of support for the program to the commissioner a few days before the panel is convened.

Media

Members of the media should be provided with a statement outlining the official college position on the topic. The statement should indicate that the college intends to seek continuation of the program and attempt to diminish the anxiety expressed by students, but should not say things that would unnecessarily upset the commissioner or members of the commission. Care should be taken to make certain that some media do not receive favored treatment about the response by the college to the commissioner.

State Commission for Higher Education

The dean and president should discuss the way the college will respond to this overture from the commissioner. Initially, a letter should be sent by the president to the commissioner indicating that the college will seek to retain the program when the president and dean appear before the hearing panel. This letter should also include some statements that would support an affirmative response from the hearing panel and the commission.

Next, the dean and president should agree upon an approach

to be taken when they appear before the hearing panel. Ideally, the president should make an opening general statement on behalf of the program and the dean should provide more specific information regarding the reasons for retaining the interior design program. The following topics should be covered during the two presentations:

- Uniqueness of the program—compared with those offered by other colleges and universities in the state.

- Strength of the program—based on comments from the consultant, alumni, accreditation bodies, and the interior design business community, among others.

- Support for the program—letters received from students, alumni, business people, legislators, and others.

- Future enrollment in the program—based on data from the college, as well as state and national figures pertaining to program enrollment and occupational outlook.

- Comparative cost information—attempts should be made to identify cost data that will demonstrate the cost-effectiveness of the program at Urbane State College compared with those at other state institutions, especially Upstate Tech.

- Comparative advantages—a listing should be prepared of advantages that would accrue to Urbane State College and the state if the program were continued rather than terminated.

The president and dean should be prepared to respond to questions after their presentations and should distribute copies of their statements to the members of the hearing panel, the commissioner, and the commissioner's staff at the conclusion of the session.

This listing of topics provides Dean Wilson with a number of options that might be considered in responding to the letter from the commissioner and the anticipated appearance before the hearing panel. (David A. Strand, Vice President and Provost, Illinois State University, Normal, Illinois.)

Both responses detail steps an institution's administration should take in dealing with the possibility of program discontinuance at the hands of a state coordinating commission. The first response (Vice President Ford) describes the extensive homework that must be effectively done to meet such a challenge. The second response (Vice President Strand) describes the roles and responsibilities of various key figures and groups in the development of an integrated plan to deal with the matter.

Although implicit in both responses, there is a dimension to dealing with state agencies that should be made explicit. Briefly put, it takes an enormous amount of time. Since state agencies want to be accountable and "amount to something," they must do something. What they do usually results in a significant increase in the workload of already hard-pressed campus administrators. This increase in workload is unlikely to be matched by increased administrative staffing to get the work done. It is a common cry that administrations are overstaffed already, and proposals to add additional positions "just to deal with the state" are unlikely to get very far.

Debatable gains likely to be realized by dealing with program duplication on a statewide basis are likely to be offset by losses in the time and attention administrators are able to bring to other pressing issues on their campuses. Believing that this leads to more effective management of the academic enterprise may depend on whether one is on a campus looking out or beyond the campus looking in. In any case, it has become a matter to which deans and provosts must commit a continually increasing proportion of their most precious resource—time.

Technology: Computers, Networking, and Bottomless Pits

Computers have profoundly changed the nature of academic management. They have made available types of data useful in decision-making that couldn't be procured before. They have also led to highly professionalized expert staff to develop and manage an institution's information system. The experts, of course, have their own language, and translation is often difficult.

The costs are enormous. Hardware, software, and professional expertise are all evolving rapidly. To keep abreast, an institution may find that resources previously committed to libraries, research equipment, laboratory and classroom space, and support are increasingly required to feed the seemingly insatiable computer network.

The advent of the computer has also produced a qualitatively new set of problems. Job descriptions of key administrators may have to be changed significantly to deal with them. The relationships between and among key administrators are likely to be reshaped, as the following case study shows.

CASE STUDY

It was the first time in years that the provost/vice president for academic affairs (VPAA) had a serious disagreement with the vice president for finance. They had worked together so well on so many other issues that it perplexed the provost that computers should now divide them. They had both agreed two years ago to a significant computer buildup on the campus, and for most of that time had combined forces to accomplish what neither of them could accomplish alone. Now they were obstinately at cross-purposes, or so it seemed, each unwilling to yield. Although the provost held his "number two on campus" in reserve on most occasions, he felt himself being drawn into a situation in which his hand could be forced. The VP for finance, after all, had served 25 years at the university and had many friends—from the faculty all the way to the governor's office.

Perhaps the big mistake, the provost mused, was not in the computer buildup but rather in the degree of networking they had both advocated. The Achilles' heel of networking—"Who has access to what?"—had became the issue they seemed unable to agree upon. They both knew that a system of security codes could be built in to permit or deny access once they agreed on workable answers to the question they posed, but they seemed utterly unable to agree on usable answers. Just as sure as the VP for finance was adamant that the faculty—or the deans either, for that matter—had no business poking around in the central financial data, so also the provost was adamant that the financial folk had no business prowling around unguided in the academic data. A rather impressive database had been built and a number of powerful systems for its manipulation installed. Although the provost and the VP for finance reeled a bit, they had even been able to manage the cost.

It looked now like it might all turn sour. What options are available through which the two can develop a workable agreement on access?

Response # 1

This is a case where apparently an information policy—particularly on access to information—had not been addressed before the technology was giving individuals options for intrusive access. What is needed is a cooperative look at the policy issues, with frank discussions among the key senior administrators, since apparently administrative databases are the problem.

Data and the information derivable from data are property. In an individual case, the use of that property may have an institutional history. At some universities, all data on faculty, students, financial and operational activities, academic programs, etc. are *closely* held. At some universities, the tradition has developed of sharing information *broadly* with the community, with the understanding that the information will be used responsibly. In a networked environment, the former is a less credible policy than the latter. Although the security system installed may be close to 100 percent effective, the availability of the potential access is an attraction for all users to resist the incorporation of sensitive information into the database.

I would assume that, first, there should be general agreement that there are "owners" of databases, with some having many people sharing in that ownership. The system should be arranged so that the owners include the only individuals who can make changes (i.e., "write" in the database). This is essential for the integrity of the data in the database. Security code protection for this should be assisted by continuous and monitored backup for the database.

I then suggest that the policy on access could go on to define at least two other classes of individuals with an interest in a given database. One would be a group of people who need to have access to information ("read only"), and would normally be in departments needing to work with information contained in the data base. A second group, with wider membership, would be individuals who need to have information derivable from the database under review. They could then have a set of "report" programs available to them that would use data in a given database to derive the information needed.

The following examples of different kinds of useful databases—and who might be in the various groups—could be helpful in assisting the two senior administrators in their formulation of an access policy.

1. A library catalogue. Cataloguers in the library should be the people having "write" access. Other library staff should have "read" access to enable them to check availability, orders, and usage, and review the database for omissions or errors, etc. Faculty, students, and other library users should have access to "report screens" that would enable them to search the database for particular book records, based on author, title, or possible key words, etc.

2. The university accounting system. Certain individuals in the financial offices (e.g., controller, budget officers, grant officers) would have to have "write" access to create or modify accounts or records, in some cases with access to only a subset of the whole database. Financial officers, auditors, etc. would need access to the database on a "read" basis, to use the information there and to check it. Faculty, department heads, and senior officers would have access to work-related reports such as their budgets and recorded transactions.

3. The student records system. The registrar's office, bursar, admissions office, financial aid office, etc. will have individuals who will be entering or modifying records, and thus have to have "write" access. Instructors will need access to limited parts of the database (about their own classes), as will deans in the various schools, and should have restricted access for "reading" of those parts of the database pertinent to their responsibilities. Other officers, students, and other faculty could have access to certain reports from the system (e.g., pattern of enrollments in courses, teaching loads in various departments, etc.).

With these examples in mind, I would propose to the two senior officers that, in fact, their interests are not really divergent. They each feel, apparently, that their own databases should be closed to individuals connected with the other, although they may also feel that *they* should have access to the other's databases. The apparent conflict in holding those views at the same time could be resolved by instituting a policy that restricted access, except for those who needed information, but followed the practice of encouraging access to general information in a format that ensured the integrity of the information. On a campus—which is a community—there should not be opposition to providing information on all aspects of the operation of the university, as long as providing that information did not violate an individual's or a group's right to privacy with respect to their own business such as salaries, personal and departmental evaluations, and related matters. (Maurice Glicksman, Provost and Dean of Faculty, Brown University, Providence, Rhode Island.)

Response # 2

As with every other industry in today's high-tech environment, higher education is irretrievably anchored to the "beauty and the beast" that is computer technology. The "beauty" is evidenced in the endless capabilities and possibilities offered by the computer in research, instruction, and administrative disciplines, while the "beast" presents a side of cybernetics that unbalances the budget, precludes privacy, and disturbs professional working relationships. Such is the case in the scenario in which a productive, cooperative relationship is threatened by the technology (the beast) that forged the partnership and produced the computer capability (the beauty).

Not to worry, for what technology creates it also controls. Our provost and financial vice president must be introduced to the concept of the proactive security system, an incredibly effective software product that provides before-the-fact security clearance at any given level of an application program. This capability provides peace of mind to the system owners by allowing them to determine who may have access to the database/data files, how often, for how long per access, and the level of detail to which access is granted. With the clear caveat that no security system is absolute and that the security system established be equal to the level of threat anticipated, our friends may once again rejoin the relationship that produced such effective results, knowing beforehand that their respective data will be secure from unauthorized access with the introduction of a proactive security product. (Joseph W. Ullman, Assistant Vice President Administrative Computing Services, University of Virginia, Charlottesville, Virginia.)

Response # 3

The dilemma faced by the two vice presidents is not unusual on campuses today. Sometimes, each party becomes too personally involved in topics, and territorial issues cloud the bigger question of what is best for the institution.

The following options might be considered by the provost/VPAA.

1. Bring in a consultant or a consulting team from off-campus to make recommendations designed to resolve the problems between the two vice presidents. Hopefully, each vice president would be willing to accept this approach and consider seriously the recommendation of the consultant(s). Professional organizations such as EDUCOM can provide people with a regional or national perspective to assist a campus in resolving problems.

2. Explore with the president and vice president for finance the establishment of academic and administrative computer advisory committees. Each committee would:

A. Include in its membership representatives from user units.

B. Report to the respective vice presidents (academic to the provost, administrative to finance).

C. Have a broad-based function, but also make recommendations regarding such items as access to data and screens as well as items of disagreement between the two vice presidents.

3. Divide the computer services of the campus into separate academic and administrative operations, but make a cost-benefit analysis before doing so.

4. Obtain minicomputers for sensitive areas in the academic units to store data and control access to the data.

5. Move the responsibility for the control of data (usually Institutional Research) to the office of the president and have the president resolve disputes.

6. Suggest to the vice president for finance that each vice president be given the opportunity to present his or her case to the president, and have the president make the final decision regarding those items over which there is disagreement between the two vice presidents.

Each of the options, or a combination, should be considered in an attempt to resolve the problems between the two vice presidents. (David A. Strand, Vice President and Provost, Illinois State University, Normal, Illinois.)

Several aspects of academic life are marked by the fact that practice often precedes the development of policy. On many campuses, computer utilization frequently fits into this category. As more sophisticated computer systems are brought to the campus, someone, somewhere will use them whether or not an adequate and enforceable access policy is in place.

Each of the responses proposes a way to deal with this dilemma. The first response (Provost Glicksman) is based on the recognition of information as property, the need to establish ownership of the various databases, and the necessity of establishing several quite different levels of access. The second response (Assistant Vice President Ullman) recommends the use of a proactive security system to determine not only levels of access but also the regulations that apply once access has been gained. The third response (Vice President Strand) lays out a half-dozen alternative ways of dealing with underlying issues.

Successful implementation of a combination of these alternatives will likely solve the immediate problem and set the stage for recognizing incipient problems as they arise. As computer technology becomes even more sophisticated, proactive security systems will be essential. So also will proactive administrators.

CHAPTER SIX
Meeting The Special Challenge

THE TASKS AND CHALLENGES before the academic officer can be almost endlessly variegated. The profusion of issues and problems is among the blessings and curses that characterize the office of the dean or provost. One significant aspect of success in these roles is the ability to switch from one item of concern to another with dispatch and without carrying the emotional burden of one set of issues or problems over into another unrelated set. The issues and problems brought to the fore in any working day come with amazing rapidity. The oft-cited blessing of "never a dull moment" is frequently accompanied by the realization that it is impossible to catch up with all the important matters one should be involved in before they are replaced with another set. It is in response to this reality that deans and provosts establish their particular style of delegating.

Nuances become extremely important both in identifying and characterizing the issues, then in formulating viable strategies for dealing with them. In each case, the question "Can I delegate this?" is complicated by the variable talents among the people to whom it might be delegated. Is the problem with the cadavers in the anatomy department a matter of academic freedom or one of poor organization and management? Since the department chair brought the problem, to whom can I refer it? Under what sets of circumstances can the academic community "do its own thing,"

161

and when must it also serve as an agent of the larger society? How do we differentiate when we are being responsive or accountable to society from those times when we are serving as an extension of society? The apparent abstractness of such questions can become quite particular when concrete issues are at hand, as the following case studies demonstrate.

Puerto Rican Studies: Tenure and Community Sensitivity

A set of special challenges can unfold when individuals in neighboring communities take an interest in activities on the campus. Emotions can run high when issues of space, lifestyle, tax support, and autonomy become inflamed and intermingled with academic matters, as academics in many urban institutions can attest. Attending and responding to the various interests of ethnic groups can be complex, as the following case study illustrates.

CASE STUDY

Within a month of becoming the new dean of arts and sciences, Henry Jones found himself increasingly preoccupied with the Eduardo Rivera case. An early appointment with Karl Schwartz, the political science chair, had provided an overview of the problem. An assistant professor of political science, Rivera offered courses in Latin American affairs with special emphasis on Puerto Rico. He had been hired six years ago after the Puerto Rican students at the eastern urban university had conducted a series of highly visible demonstrations in an attempt to secure the establishment of a department of Puerto Rican studies.

The university had not agreed to their demand to establish such a department. Instead, it had offered to hire a Spanish-speaking instructor in order to add a Latin American emphasis to the political science department. The students had accepted the counterproposal on the condition that they be represented on the search committee. After further discussion, the university had agreed. Several interviews later, Rivera had been hired.

Other, more prominent scholars of Latin America had turned up in the search process, one or two with fairly significant research records. However, the students had insisted on someone with a Puerto Rican background, so Rivera's name had been moved to the top of the list, even though he lacked the doctorate. At the time of the last interview, the university had indicated that it expected Rivera to complete the terminal degree within a "reasonable period of time." Rivera had agreed and so had been hired.

Other things had seemed to intervene, however, and six years later Rivera had still not received his degree. A call was made by Schwartz to Rivera's dissertation adviser to learn what progress had been made. Very little, it appeared. Schwartz asked the dissertation advisor if an extension was possible for Rivera. The advisor indicated that such extensions were contrary to university policy and that her department was about ready to drop Rivera from the roster because of his inactivity.

Later, in talking with Rivera, Schwartz had stressed the importance of the degree and had observed that Rivera had little chance of tenure without it. In response, Rivera had commented on the various responsibilities he felt to the Puerto Rican community in the area. Community service was an important professional obligation, Rivera had continued, and the university had for too long neglected the Spanish-speaking population. He did not deny the importance of the degree, he added, but he did feel strongly that traditional academic requirements were irrelevant to good teaching and community service.

Still, he had agreed to renew his attention to the dissertation, and Schwartz felt relieved. Rivera subsequently made some progress, but not nearly enough, for the dissertation was still unfinished. It was not long after the chair's conversation with Rivera that a committee of students called upon Dean Jones to convey their appreciation for Rivera. He was an outstanding professor, they observed, and the university was fortunate to have him. They had heard that his tenure status was uncertain, and they hoped that the university recognized the unfortunate publicity and lasting harm a negative decision would be sure to create.

The following week, a delegation of community leaders made many of the same points, and concluded that the university might be displaying a form of racism were it to refuse to recognize the importance of university involvement with the Hispanic community.

Jones felt himself over a barrel. On the one hand, he felt strongly that the university needed stronger ties to the nearby, growing, Spanish-speaking population. On the other hand, making a positive tenure recommendation in the absence of the terminal degree was sure to send the wrong message to other arts and sciences departments. Jones knew that the provost would expect a well-defended recommendation, either way.

How might Jones best deal with this matter?

Response # 1

In the world of academe there is a generally accepted model for a faculty member. The words and phrases may vary from institution to institution, but essentially each faculty member is expected to exhibit the following characteristics: teaching ability; scholarly activity; contribution to the profession; participation in the affairs of the department, school, and college; and public service. Effectiveness in the classroom and good academic relationships with students both in and out of the classroom are the sine qua non for every person holding rank in any respectable department. None of the characteristics seems to be sufficient by themselves to offset lack of teaching ability. But teaching alone is not enough. It can never be a substitute for the proper credentials and the research, writing, and scholarly presentations that will enable an individual to stay at the cutting edge of his or her discipline and maintain enthusiasm, zest, and commitment over the long haul.

Many of our colleges and universities are still filled with older faculty who have justified their existence because of excellence in teaching and community service in the broadest sense. They often do not possess the appropriate terminal degree and they usually exhibit little or no scholarly activity. They are often popular with students and have a good political base because of involvement with the bargaining agent and/or the governance structure. They have been successful in their own eyes. But all too often we see in these same individuals interesting presentations in the classroom of the same ideas, concepts, philosophies, and points of view that they were presenting twenty-five years ago. They have not matured in their disciplines. They have not grown, developed, or enlarged their scope and vision. They continue to cheat their students, and the tragedy is that neither they nor their students realize it.

Advanced study, research, and continued involvement with the foremost thought within the discipline are essential if each professor is to share with his or her students all that they expect and deserve. Even depth of study and research are not enough. Thoughts, ideas, theories, and new information must be committed to writing before they are crystallized and pure. Fuzzy thinking and hazy ideas are all too troublesome until they are digested and placed on paper or shared in a formal oral presentation. The requirements of research, writing, and scholarly presentations are not just hurdles and hoops for young overburdened faculty. They are not just outworn badges of some elite professional society. They are the tools of the trade for those who aspire to the pinnacles of academe. If our colleges and universities are to be respected institutions of higher learning, those who are influential in matters of hiring, tenuring, and promoting must never lose sight of the importance of these expectations and requirements.

The doctorate or the appropriate terminal degree is only the first step along this path, but it is a necessary first step. No faculty member today, given almost universal access to advanced higher education, should be permitted to join the tenured faculty ranks without this prerequisite.

Henry Jones's decision is a difficult one, but the choice is clear. He must not permit Rivera to gain tenure. Jones will pay a heavy price for this decision, but in the long term the decision will be respected and he will also know it is the right one. The pressures from students, faculty supporters, the community, and others will be intense. Grievances, civil rights actions, and even lawsuits may ensue. However, Henry Jones has to stand firm.

One must remember that the primary role of a college or university is to meet the educational needs of society. The university is not a social institution. It should try to be responsive to social and economic needs of society, but it must always keep its eye on its primary role. It cannot reconstruct society. It cannot be a major provider for the social welfare needs of people. Because many people do not understand that, there will be cries of outrage directed toward Henry Jones. The 1960s and 1970s, when many tried to blunt and change the major purpose of the university, are still vivid in our memories. Fortunately, we are back on track, and the Henry Jones' of the academic world will prevail. (Gordon I. Goewey, retired. Formerly Vice President for Academic Affairs and Provost, Trenton State College, Trenton, New Jersey.)

Response # 2

The university probably made a mistake when it decided to hire Eduardo Rivera primarily because of his Puerto Rican background even though he lacked the doctorate. However, since Rivera has established a record of outstanding teaching and is a valuable member of the college faculty, a reasonable effort should be made to maintain him.

I do not believe the university should compromise its standards for granting tenure by recommending Rivera for tenure without the doctorate degree. To do so would indeed send the wrong message to the arts and sciences faculty.

The university should arrange to grant Professor Rivera a year's leave of absence with pay to complete his doctorate. This leave should be granted with the clear understanding that Rivera will return to the university the following year under a terminal contract if he does not have the degree in hand. If a formal leave of absence cannot be granted, Mr. Rivera should be relieved of all teaching and committee assignments for the academic year in which he is given time to complete the degree.

Minority faculty are often expected to wear too many hats. It was perhaps unwise for the university to hire Mr. Rivera and then expect him to fulfill routine academic obligations while also serving as an ambassador to the Puerto Rican students and to the larger community. The university bears some of the responsibility for the situation that now exists. But Rivera also bears some for not completing the doctorate. A leave of absence or full release time with the requirement that Rivera finish the doctorate seems a fair approach to resolving the problem. If it is made absolutely clear to Rivera that he must finish the doctorate and he fails to do so in the allotted time, the university will have shown good faith before terminating him. (Barbara L. Carter, Vice President for Academic Affairs and Provost, Spelman College, Atlanta, Georgia.)

The first respondent (former Vice President Goewey) summarizes nicely the tradition regarding faculty competencies and accomplishments. Within this context, he argues, the decision before the dean is clear. The second respondent (Vice President Carter) offers somewhat different counsel, as she directs our attention to the many expectations institutions have placed upon their minority faculty members—expectations frequently well in excess of those for other faculty members. Such expectations should be recognized in the promotion and tenure process, alongside the more traditional academic credentials, and opportunities provided for meeting them.

In this case the dean must be prepared to address the issues of favoritism, exception, and precedent. The favoritism issue can be easily handled. The problem of violating established procedures or of making exceptions to them may be more difficult to address. Skillful responses to these matters can defuse subsequent arguments that precedents have been established.

Regional and Specialized Accreditation: Who's Next?

Accreditation activities play a major role in the lives of academic officers. Some find the activities to be quite rewarding, providing a structured opportunity to review the status of academic programs and their progress toward appropriate goals, then later to check perceptions and judgments with knowledgeable others from outside the campus. Other academic officers, however, find accreditation activities to be more frustrating, involving either expensive and time-consuming confirmations of the obvious or yielding expectations of the impossible. A steady stream of such activities can be quite frustrating and complicated by differences between the value systems of accrediting agencies and the university. The following case study suggests some of the difficulties that may arise.

CASE STUDY

VPAA Jim Steadfast, in a moment of whimsy, thought of installing a number-dispensing machine at his receptionist's desk similar to those he had seen in bakeries. Then, when the next accreditation group showed up he could have the receptionist tell them to take a number and have a seat until it was called. Every time he turned around, it seemed there was one group or another proposing to accredit a particular program.

He expected the regionals, of course. Dealing with them was one of the costs of doing business. He had his doubts about the value of the so-called self-study the institution had to construct. At times, it seemed mainly to be a protracted hassle, but he always went along because it was the lesser of two evils. Government inspection would be far worse. Except for an occasionally arrogant visitor, it normally went well, and he was usually pleased with the outcome. Indeed, once in a while he even found some of their "suggestions" useful.

The specialized accrediting groups were something else again. If it wasn't music, it was art. If it wasn't dental assisting, it was interior decorating. The list seemed endless. The costs were usually considerable and the results of dubious value. Often, the outcome was simply a protracted pitch for more resources, with little regard for where they would come from or for the balance of the university.

Things had come to a head with a recent report from the engineering group. The visiting team had praised the faculty for their commitment to students as well as for their continuing professional involvement. The curriculum had been characterized as adequate-to-strong. The team's concerns had focused on the decreasing level of institutional funds committed to library resources and to equipment purchase. Indeed, the report had described the laboratory equipment as becoming obsolete at an alarming rate. The insufficiency of funds might be connected with the decrease in research productivity of the faculty, the report noted, and both matters were of sufficient importance that continuation of accreditation was in jeopardy. At least, that was the impression Steadfast got upon reading the report and talking with the engineering faculty and dean.

The difficulty was that the equipment and library budgets were already exhausted and no increases were scheduled or in sight for the next few years. The economic turndown in the state had left bare budgets all around. What little discretionary funds were available had been publicly committed by the president to securing AACSB accreditation for the graduate school of business. At least, she had gone on record at the fall convocation that the university's next step in its "reach toward excellence" was to achieve this AACSB stature.

Steadfast could see no way the university could spring for the funds that the engineering folks were suggesting and also secure the expensive faculty that AACSB would require.

What options does Jim Steadfast have at this point?

Response # 1

As may be all too typical with reports from specialized accreditation bodies, the report from the engineering accreditation group (ABET) points out what it considers to be significant deficiencies in the resources available to the engineering program. Vice President Steadfast needs to examine the report closely and, in consultation with the college of engineering, reach a conclusion as to whether the report is accurate in its conclusions. If Steadfast concludes that the description presented in the report is indeed accurate, he then has two options: secure the funds in order to maintain the accreditation of the engineering program, or discontinue the engineering program altogether. The latter is an unfortunate option, but an engineering program without ABET accreditation is not a viable alternative for any university.

In choosing between these two alternatives, Vice President Steadfast needs to refer to the university's priorities for its academic programs. These, no doubt, have been arrived at through "strategic planning." If the engineering programs have a high priority, Vice President Steadfast has only the first option; he must secure funds in order to maintain the accreditation for the programs in engineering. If engineering is viewed as a minor program at the institution, the second option is available, and the engineering programs could be phased out over a number of years.

Let's assume that engineering programs have a high priority, having enjoyed considerable support from the students and local employers of the university's graduates. The question, then, is "Where can Steadfast obtain money to continue accreditation?" Perhaps the most obvious answer lies in the effort to obtain AACSB accreditation for the college of business. While the president has made a commitment to move in this direction, I note that the university has ABET accreditation but not AACSB accreditation. It would be folly to proceed on a path that would surely result in the loss of ABET accreditation and not guarantee AACSB accreditation. I propose that Steadfast pursue the path of, first, maintaining ABET accreditation, then turning toward AACSB accreditation.

To do this, Steadfast will have to be aware of the support in the local business community for AACSB accreditation. If this support is significant, it may be very difficult to convince the president to divert funds presently earmarked for AACSB accreditation to maintain the accreditation of the engineering programs. However, the potential may exist for support in the business community for ABET accreditation as well as for AACSB accreditation.

In summary, Steadfast needs to do his homework on the issues and then be prepared to approach the president with very cogent arguments for diverting funds from AACSB accreditation to ABET accreditation. I believe he should resist the strong temptation to suggest that the university forego specialized accreditation. While these are costly and troublesome, certain programs are not viable without accreditation. In most states, engineers cannot obtain a professional engineer's license if they have not graduated from an accredited program.

It is possible that Steadfast and the dean of the college do not agree with the conclusions reached by the accrediting body. The options then available to Steadfast are more complex. He needs to examine the likely outcome of the report. Is it certain that the report will lead to loss of accreditation? Is it possible that he may be able to present additional data to the team such that they will modify the report? Is it possible for the institution to appeal to the accrediting organization as a whole? It will be very difficult for Steadfast and the university to accept the report as accurate and not make any changes. Obviously, this would lead to loss of accreditation. If, however, he can point out that the report is grossly inaccurate, there may be a chance to have the accreditation continued in spite of the report. I would say that this last option is a long shot because in most situations it has been my experience that the accrediting agency accurately describes the circumstances on a campus. (Donald E. Bowen, Vice President for Academic Affairs, Southwest Missouri State University, Springfield, Missouri.)

Response # 2

Jim Steadfast, Vice President for Academic Affairs at Cynical University, is probably not an isolated example of a chief academic officer caught between the apparently conflicting demands of specialized and regional accrediting agencies and the dwindling resources of his own university. His attitude toward the accreditation groups—ranging from impatience to "better this evil than an even greater one"—has very likely communicated itself to the deans and heads of the various groups competing for resources. It is not surprising, then, to find that Jim Steadfast's engineering dean is tightening the screws with regard to equipment.

Since most accreditation teams are composed of ordinary mortals who have roots in institutions not unlike Cynical U., they are doubtless all too familiar with the most common institutional illnesses, ranging from Borderline Budget Crunch to Terminal Tightening of the Belt. At the risk of offering nothing more than a sugar-coated placebo, honesty might actually be the best policy in this instance. Jim Steadfast and his president should take the accreditation report seriously, allow the engineering faculty to bask in the compliments they have been paid, and commiserate (publicly, if necessary) over the sad state of the equipment and the very serious needs that have been confirmed rather than discovered by the accreditation team.

A long-range plan should be made and discussed with the dean of engineering, other equipment users, and heads of divisions, including the dean of the school of business, and a time table for remedying deficiencies should be provided to the accreditation team. The team will be persuaded by an honest plan and by the willingness of various university divisions to take an institutional view and make the compromises necessary to ensure that the legitimate needs of all sectors get the attention they deserve, even if they cannot get the immediate action they would all like.

When the accreditation team has considered the timetable for equipment purchases and has reaccredited Cynical U., and the business school has received the imprimatur of the AACSB, the university might consider changing its name to Utopia University. (Hannah Goldberg, Provost and Academic Vice President, Wheaton College, Norton, Massachusetts.)

Both responses recognize that accreditation reports need to be taken seriously. The first response (Vice President Bowen) describes a number of options for dealing with the difficulties presented in the case study. The second response (Provost Goldberg) reminds us that many problems that seem insoluble in the short run may become amenable to solution if the time frame is extended. An effective long-range planning process and the resultant long-range plan may be useful in solving a number of problems along with the one presented here.

Some prestigious institutions believe that they do not need specialized or programmatic accreditation to support or bolster their reputations. However, for accreditation to function as the main mechanism of self-regulation, these institutions should probably pay more attention to ways in which they can contribute to a viable and helpful accrediting community. The alternative to accreditation, increasing government regulation, should be a concern in all types of institutions.

In any case, accreditation—both regional and specialized—is not going to go away. Deans and provosts recognize this fact and somehow make room in their minds to deal with the consequences.

Research and Public Service: Young Turks and the Old Guard

A number of problems that occur on college and university campuses are basically definitional in character. One or more groups persist in misunderstanding one another or not even hearing one another because they are using different sets of definitions to consider an issue. So long as this situation endures, it is unlikely that they can come to agreement on policy matters of importance to them and, hence, to the institution. The following case study raises some of the difficulties likely to develop when two faculty groups have different views on the definition of research and public service.

CASE STUDY

The campus was having a difficult time coming to terms on a definition of research and public service. After prolonged debate, the faculty senate had, by a very narrow margin, passed a patch-work-quilt set of definitions. As the campus process worked, sen-ate items having a bearing on academic affairs came to the VPAA, who took them to the Deans' Council for advice before action was taken. Action meant either approval, disapproval, or referral back to the senate for more work. This time, the Deans' Council was no more united than the faculty.

New to the campus, VPAA Thomas Slaight wasn't particularly concerned about the process. He was concerned, however, about the issues involved. As far as he could tell, there was a clean split between the Young Turks and the old guard on how research and public service were to be defined. The relationship to tenure and promotion decisions was clear, and the younger faculty were pressing hard for greater recognition of their accomplishments. More than decisions about individuals rode on the outcome be-cause budgets, space allocation, positions, secretarial support, and several other things were tied to a department's research and public service activities. An annual performance report was made, and the VPAA adjusted the resources available to each college dean on the basis, in part at least, of the research and public service performance of each dean's departments.

The Young Turks held strictly to a definition based on outside funding. If someone else was willing to pay for it, they argued, it was clearly meritorious. In support, they cited the president, who was urging all departments to increase their grants and con-tract activity in nearly every on-campus speech he made.

The old guard's view was considerably softer. They held to the notion that if an individual faculty member considered what he or she was doing to be research or public service, it ought to be included in the annual report. The Young Turks wanted all on-campus committee work to be excluded as being merely in-ternal housekeeping serving no one but themselves. The old guard insisted that the house, after all, had to be kept, and the faculty had to keep it lest the administration fill the vacuum and further reduce the faculty role in what was euphemistically called "gov-ernance."

The divisions were clear and the debate heated. An additional complication was that neither group had developed performance criteria with anything like outcome measures. While neither side commanded a clear majority on the deans' council, the side that seemed to prevail had no sympathy with the faculty senate's definitions.

How would you advise Tom to handle this subject?

Response # 1

Academic administration is always a delicate balance between firm leadership and group decision-making, usually thought of as collegiality. The definitions of research and public service are very important for the institution for they will heavily influence the activity of the faculty, and thus the direction of the campus, for years to come.

The central issue of this case is how to provide the necessary academic leadership so that workable definitions are developed while honoring the tradition of collegiality. For difficult issues such as this one, the leadership must come from the chief executive officer—in this case, the president. Apparently, the president had given a clear signal through his recent speeches that more activity in the pursuit of grants and contracts was desirable. Following the president's lead, the vice president for academic affairs must communicate to the faculty that grants and contracts activity must become a more important factor in resource allocation decisions as well as in personnel decisions. Any workable definition of research and public service, therefore, would have to reflect this greater emphasis.

Collegiality implies significant faculty participation in decision-making, and this is very important on a college campus. Vice President Slaight, therefore, should be very concerned about the process. Collegiality has already been accomplished by the faculty senate, more so by its deliberations than its final recommendation. The principle of collegiality was further honored by the deliberations of the Deans' Council.

At this point, I would recommend the following sequence of steps to the vice president. First, thank the faculty senate for its work, while acknowledging the difficulty of the task. Next, inform the faculty that the senate's definitions need greater cohesion and clarity and that he will appoint a task force to develop this cohesiveness and clarity by working intensely for a short period of time—say, one month. The task force should be small—perhaps five or seven members—and composed of persons from the senate, the Deans' Council, and the general faculty. The vice president's charge to the task force should be to develop the senate definitions into a cohesive and workable statement incorporating both points of view, but emphasizing the importance of grants and contracts. "Workable" in this context not only means clarity, but also sufficient specificity so that the document can be used in developing appropriate performance criteria.

This approach would accomplish several things. It would honor the principle of collegiality by further developing the senate document. It would permit the VPAA to exert some needed leadership by choosing the members of the task force and giving it his charge. This approach would also move the campus toward closure on the issue because this small group would be much more likely to arrive at a consensus than would the full senate, and the task force would have a fixed, short time-frame for completing the work. Finally, it would provide for a high probability of acceptance by the academic community because of the broad-based participation, and because the final outcome would be a workable compromise of the two extreme positions, which would permit gradual change toward the new emphasis called for by the president. (Mickey L. Burnim, Vice Chancellor for Academic Affairs, North Carolina Central University, Durham, North Carolina.)

Response # 2

Patchwork has provided some of the best examples ever seen of the art of quilting. Each piece is individually pleasing aesthetically but hardly sufficient to provide warmth. Each piece has to be of the same size and used but once, so that a separate pattern within the whole is not suggested. Analogously, the problem with the senate's definitions is probably not that they are too general, but that they are too specific of individual's self-interests, with the Young Turks and the old guard both demanding that the VPAA use more of their "patches" in the quilt.

None of the VPAA's choices as stated will meet the desired end, but that end needs first to be redefined and expanded. There are at least three related tasks to be accomplished: definition of research and public service; development of performance criteria complete with outcome measures based on the definitions; and a rethinking of the relationship between the college's performances and resource allocation. The total task is of such a mag-

nitude that it is best handled by a body representative of the
senate and the deans chaired by the VPAA, rather than by any
single, larger group—the senate and the deans' council as groups
do not appear to work toward consensus anyway. The senate and
council representatives are responsible both to and for their constituencies; the governance process is not necessarily violated in
that all bodies appropriately involved in an academic matter are
present. All three entities must understand the interrelatedness
of the issues and each other's needs. The senate must represent
all of their colleagues equally, so that the strengths and abilities
of all faculty in research and public service can be appropriately
recognized by the dean who will be charged finally with applying
performance criteria in such a way that the VPAA can allocate
resources evenhandedly.

Ideally, the senate would provide broad, inclusive definitions
of research and public service. Given these definitions, deans
would provide specificity via annual performance "contracts" with
each faculty member in his or her college in such a way as to set
clear expectations based on the abilities and interests of each faculty member and the needs of the institution. The VPAA would
then allocate resources based on the dean's annual reports of
projected faculty performance in these areas for the coming year,
rather than on past performances, so that resource allocation supports planned activity instead of rewarding accomplishments.
(Daniel R. Hoeber, Vice President for Academic Affairs, Mercy
College of Detroit, Detroit, Michigan.)

Both responses emphasize the need for additional input. The
first response (Vice Chancellor Burnim) suggests appointing a task
force with a short reporting time to secure the additional advice.
The second response (Vice President Hoeber) calls for a similar
group, places the VPAA as chair, and expands the charge beyond
refinement of the senate's original document. An interesting aspect
of both responses is the avoidance of the temptation to have the
VPAA or president decide the matter. As the respondents point
out, it will be necessary to achieve a high degree of ownership
among the faculty, chairs, and deans for the new procedures to
be effective.

Linking the definitions to annual performance contracts and
allocating to fund future expectations seems to be a hopeful way

of getting on with the president's mandate for more research. Rewarding past activity may not be as strong a performance incentive as funding the future.

Secretarial Problems

Deans and provosts rely on an effective office staff to insure a smooth flow of business through their offices. This supporting staff may be one individual in a small institution or several in a larger one. Support staff in the academic affairs area are likely to have responsibility for monitoring budgets; auditing space, personnel, and schedule records; maintaining a smooth paper flow through the office; and presenting a welcoming milieu to those constituencies—internal and external—who contact or visit the office.

Support staff represent the dean and/or provost, and hence the institution, before these constituencies. Their effect upon student satisfaction and retention can be enormous. Secretaries and administrative assistants in the dean's and/or provost's office as well as those in the registrar's, financial aid, and business offices can help to make students feel either that "somebody cares" or that they are being ignored. Support staff can be equally influential with faculty and department chairs, earning either a positive and helpful reputation or one of indifference or even of unsavory and inappropriate status and power games.

Academic and other institutional officers need to be aware of the importance of their support staff, and treat them accordingly. Even in the best of circumstances, there may be times when they will require the personal attention of the dean or provost, as the following case study shows.

CASE STUDY

From the dean's perspective, Sarah's work as his secretary was simply superb. As dean, Joe had told her as much several times. Sarah was marvelous on the telephone, making each caller feel especially important and remaining unperturbed when several calls arrived at the same moment. Visitors were cordially received and thoughtfully attended when meetings elsewhere made Joe late for appointments. Sarah's typing was accurate and fast and her English usage was impeccable. Most impressive was her ability to anticipate what needed to be done next on the different projects the dean had underway. Sarah was smart, but had not fallen into the cynicism and ennui that he had seen overtake other intelligent people in support positions.

It was with considerable dismay, therefore, that Joe listened to the complaints from two new junior faculty members. According to them, Sarah was condescending and manipulative. She seemed to have little time for them, and when she was available it was more to be directive than to be helpful. It seemed hardly possible that the three of them were talking about the same person.

Afterward, he checked with a couple of department heads with whom he felt reasonably comfortable. To his surprise, they confirmed the complaints. Noting that they had never themselves been treated except in the most courteous manner, they observed that their own departmental secretaries did not seem to enjoy the same congenial reception. In fact, they both had noticed increasingly significant glances and lengthy hesitations when Sarah's name came up in conversation or when their secretaries had activities that required interaction with her. The word "favoritism" was mentioned with considerable disdain.

All of this was news to the dean, and it was difficult to realize that the person upon whom he had come to depend so heavily could, in fact, be perceived by others in such an uncomplimentary light. To be sure, he did allow her to leave at 4:30 in the afternoons rather than at 5, as others on the staff did, but she more than made up by arriving early in the morning. The complaints must simply be petty jealousy, he thought, but he wondered whether he should do something about them.

How would you advise the dean?

Response # 1

The dean should be aware that his secretary, Sarah, serves him and the office of the deanship in two important ways. She must be effective and efficient in the technical aspects of her role, which involves work for the dean and work directly associated with staff, instructors, and administrators. Equally important, she projects the image of the deanship. In this capacity she must be the model of discreet, courteous, professional behavior.

The dean's first step is to talk in confidence with each of his chairs to determine whether earlier critical comments about Sarah's treatment of subordinates is accurate and is substantiated across the college. The dean should be careful to seek specific information about specific cases in which other personnel have found Sarah's behavior to be offensive.

The dean's next step is to assess the evidence he has gathered from chairs and to determine the seriousness of this evidence. We note that he had previous critical information about Sarah from two junior faculty and at least two chairs.

Whether the evidence regarding Sarah's behavior is critical or not, the dean should meet with her now. Without revealing specific sources or names, he should discuss openly but gently those issues that have been raised about her behavior. It may be that other people's perceptions of her behavior are different from her view of the behavior; nevertheless, it is important that Sarah be made aware of the image she is projecting. At this point, taking into consideration the evidence the dean has assessed, he and Sarah must plan means through which changed behavior on her part will lead to changed perceptions by those who criticize her. The degree of Sarah's behavioral change will have to vary with the nature and validity of evidence available.

It is not wise personnel policy to provide continuing preferential treatment to any staff member. Sarah should keep the same office hours as the rest of the staff. It may be that the dean wants to introduce a "flex schedule." That's fine so long as all staff members have the opportunity to participate in it.

The dean should not postpone action in this matter. Fair assessment followed by fair decisions and actions will prevent headaches down the road. (Paul Ford, Vice President for Academic Affairs, Western Washington University, Bellingham, Washington.)

Response # 2

The morale and efficiency of the support staff are critical to the overall campus operation. Much of the work of every campus requires communication between the department chairpersons, the faculties, their staffs, and the dean's office. Since Sarah is the focal point for virtually all communications with the dean's office, a real or perceived problem with Sarah could be very detrimental. If her attitude and behavior in dealing with others on the campus really are such that many persons are offended or alienated, then the dean must take steps to correct her attitude and behavior. If, on the other hand, the problem derives from the perception of others that Sarah receives preferential treatment, then the dean needs to deal with whatever is contributing to that perception.

The dean should take some comfort in the knowledge that this problem is a common one. Bright efficient staff persons who have amassed a lot of experience performing their jobs often know considerably more about procedures and policies than do faculty members, especially new ones, and other campus administrators and staff. The reports of Sarah's being condescending, manipulative, and directive may simply be reactions to her attempts to get persons to follow established policies and procedures.

From the case, it appears that the problem has not yet had much impact on campus efficiency, though the potential is there. It is quite likely that the dean can solve this problem by doing three things. First, he should have a heart-to-heart talk with Sarah, explaining to her that the working relationships between the dean's office and other offices and individuals on campus must be continuously nurtured so that the work of the campus can be done without having to worry about personalities, hurt feelings, and the like. He should explain to her that all visitors and callers to the office are to be treated courteously and with the respect due persons who are important to the institution. This includes faculty, students, staff, and all visitors to the campus. I would advise Joe not to let this talk take on an accusatory tone, for the truth may be that Sarah's treatment of others really has been exemplary. In any case, this talk is likely to have its greatest effect if it is done so as not to put Sarah on the defensive.

The second thing that Joe can do to correct any mistaken notions about the appropriate way to treat new faculty members and other support staff members is to set a very careful example. It is possible that Sarah's attitude and treatment of all persons who come in contact with the office are reflections of how she sees the dean react to them. The dean must make sure that he always treats faculty, staff, and others with the utmost respect and courtesy.

guage traditions from which they came. It wasn't just the usual case of competing academic specialties. After all, many departments have to endure that. In art, painters and art educators frequently don't get on well with one another. In music, instrumentalists and vocalists live in different worlds. In biology, the molecular and organismal folks often disagree. So it goes throughout much of the academic spectrum. No, the problem here was deeper. Among the professors of Spanish was an Argentinian, a Puerto Rican, a Castillian from Madrid, and a senior much-published linguist from Kansas City. The French group included a Gaullist, two from Quebec, and a French-speaking African black. The German group was rather homogeneous. They all came from the same graduate school, all had the same point of view, and all thought their non-Germanic colleagues were, to say the least, strange and uncooperative.

A third layer of the problem was that the chair, quite effective in the more halycon days of his mid-career a decade ago, no longer commanded the respect of his colleagues. He was, in fact, rather baffled by their behavior. He viewed their outbursts as childlike and had tried several parenting techniques with them. Nothing worked. His interventions seemed only to make matters worse.

The dean knew that the chair had to be replaced, but no one else in the department seemed to be a suitable candidate, and the dean didn't have an open position he could transfer to foreign language in order to recruit from the outside. Nor could he wait much longer. An argument had broken out during the multiyear all-university committee effort to revise the general education program, which could prove embarrassing. Some faculty were holding to the position that all undergraduates should have two years of the same language; others argued for only one year. The dean feared the consequences of having the all-university committee see the dishevelment that had infected the foreign language faculty, and he certainly didn't want them to see and hear the probably ineffective testimony of the chair. If this wasn't all handled carefully, he could lose a foreign language requirement altogether—and he certainly didn't want that to happen.

The dean reviewed his options. He could (1) live with the situation and hope for the best; (2) assign the chair duties to one of his other chairpersons, perhaps from one of the sciences; (3)

temporarily install himself as chair and impose an academic equivalent to martial law; or (4) pick one of the warring parties in the department to take on the job of chair. He had recently read of a dean who had placed a dysfunctional department into "receivership." He wondered if he should do likewise.

How would you advise the dean in this situation?

Response # 1

Receivership is a temporary solution—a holding pattern—that should only be used when a longer-term solution is being developed. This is a case where good longer-term solutions don't seem to be available. It is not possible to recruit for a new outside chair. Nor does there seem to be the possibility of terminating or reassigning faculty to other departments.

I believe the best approach in this situation is to pick one of the warring parties in the department to take on the job of chair. The individual selected to chair the department should be selected primarily on the basis of his or her ability to speak to the all-university committee on the value of maintaining a two-year language requirement. The chair should be further charged with the responsibility of trying to reduce tension and conflict in the department. (Barbara L. Carter, Vice President for Academic Affairs and Provost, Spelman College, Atlanta, Georgia.)

Response # 2

Receiverships are dangerous. Sometimes they work, when all else has failed, but frequently they cause as many problems as they solve. Dean Glass has some other possibilities he should examine first.

Glass's problem may be a program opportunity disguised as a personnel crisis. Tinkering with the department's leadership—which is what all the options, including the receivership notion, amount to—is unlikely to resolve the crisis because the faculty does not want to be led. It appears to be a tired and cantankerous group, held together only by its common sour disposition and trapped in an unstimulating and uninteresting academic environment. Department members entertain themselves with petty in-fighting, and new leadership would only provide a new target for the brickbats.

The key to solving Glass's problem may lie in an unexamined assumption: "He could lose a foreign language requirement altogether—and he certainly didn't want that to happen." Why not? The requirement—and the courses it supports—is probably as stale and tired as the faculty, and the relentless drudgery of teaching elementary language to an audience of unwilling students may be central to the personal and professional unhappiness of the faculty.

Why not try something dramatic to snap the department out of its lethargy? Here's a possibility: Drop the language requirement altogether, and install a really attractive study-abroad program for which intermediate language-competence is a prerequisite. For the term abroad, send one of the professors with a group of students. Give him or her responsibility for some of the teaching while abroad, as well as for hiring additional instruction on-site and for making bed-and-board arrangements, the former through a local university, the latter through one of the many organizations like Experiment in International Living that specialize in placing young people.

Most of the faculty members in Dean Glass's department are foreign-born; they would probably welcome the opportunity to return "home," and they would no doubt find the change of pace refreshing and challenging. At a minimum, they would be out of the local bearpit for a term. It should be possible to work out the costs of the program in such a way that student tuition or, in a public institution, the appropriate allocation, will cover all the costs including transportation, living, instruction, etc., and leave a little left for overhead. Students will be better motivated to study foreign languages, and it is likely that faculty members will take more interest in the challenges of elementary language instruction. Good "marketing" of the program should make it popular and result in maintaining a good proportion of the foreign language enrollments.

Faculty members, preoccupied in developing separate study-abroad programs in Argentina, Quebec, Puerto Rico, Spain, Germany, and elsewhere, will probably be less tempted to engage in negative, cynical, and otherwise unhappy behavior. It is possible that the leadership problem will remain. If so, Dean Glass can avoid the painful authoritarian decision to form a receivership by designating someone—perhaps one of the existing faculty members, perhaps someone outside the department—as "Director of Study Abroad," and allowing that person to "work into" the department, assuming leadership gradually, and as invisibly as possible.

Most people do not enjoy misbehaving, and we can assume that is true of the faculty members in Dean Glass's foreign language department. They usually will embrace reasonable alternatives, especially ones that make them feel valued and important. Receiverships usually carry exactly the opposite message. They insult faculty members and deepen the downward spiral of unproductive behavior. Dean Glass can avoid the receivership and at the same time breathe some new life into the college's foreign language program. (Charles S. Olton, Vice President and Dean of the Faculty, Barnard College, Columbia University, New York, New York.)

Response # 3

Civil wars tend to flare when a potentially bellicose nation does not have an external enemy or, at least, an internal objective that demands cooperation. In this case study, the foreign language department faculty were so occupied during the 1960s that, although individuals may not have gotten along, each had matters of greater import than expending efforts on petty differences. Although Dean Glass cannot turn back the hands of time, he can do something about the amount of time the faculty have on their hands that they are presently spending on in-fighting.

As a first step, though, he must relieve the present chair, who is not necessarily the cause of the problem, but seems at a loss to solve it. Appointing a chair from one of the other camps would be taken as a vote of confidence by the dean for that faction's position. There is little to be gained and much to be lost by appointing, for example, the chair of biology to this post. Why detract from one discipline in the hope of improving another? Dean Glass should assume the duties as chair for one academic year, and could do so without imposing an academic equivalent of martial law.

Rather, the dean will serve as the one who will lead the faculty into battle against a worthy and formidable opponent—a revised general education curriculum that may well annihilate an already weakened foreign language department. Without a united front on this particular issue, the faculty will, as the dean perceived, be an easy prey for the all-university committee. The dean, then, serves as a sort of single-purpose chair for one year to see that the faculty come together on one project that has nothing to do with internal personality conflicts. Of course, early on the dean needs to make it unmistakably clear that, far from being the enemy, the students can be a powerful ally, so that maltreatment that had been going on in the past is to stop immediately.

Dean Glass should explain, upon assuming the chair, that he felt it unfair to appoint a faculty member with no experience as a chair to that position and also expect that person to assume leadership in the considerable task of addressing the general education question. Also, he should indicate that, having worked so closely with the faculty in this one year, he would have a much better sense of whom to appoint as the next chair.

I would bet on the linguist from Kansas City. (Daniel R. Hoeber, Vice President for Academic Affairs, Mercy College of Detroit, Detroit, Michigan.)

The three responses to this case study are quite different. The first (Vice President Carter) suggests appointing an individual from one of the warring parties to be chair, with the individual selected on the basis of his or her ability to handle the issue of the foreign language requirement. The second response (Vice President Olton) sees that "tinkering with the department's leadership" may not provide a solution no matter who is selected. He recommends letting the foreign language requirement go, and developing instead an exciting study-abroad program to rejuvenate the department. The third response (Vice President Hoeber) suggests going for receivership, with the dean serving as chair on a temporary basis. With the dean serving as a "single-purpose chair," the department's position in the battle over the foreign language requirement is likely to be strengthened and time provided for the situation to settle and new leadership become visible.

These responses clearly show that experienced academics can and do think in diverse ways about the problems/opportunities they encounter. Which of the three ways of thinking about the situation posed by this case study would work out best on a given campus, of course, can not be ascertained from the information given. Many more variables would have to be considered in setting a particular strategy in motion.

The best device the academy has ever found for ensuring its future in such matters is to engage the attention of experienced and capable academic leaders, managers, and administrators— that is to say, deans and provosts. If they didn't exist, it would truly be necessary for the faculty to invent them. Fortunately for the academy, they do exist in considerable number, as the responses to this and the preceding case studies make abundantly clear.

CHAPTER SEVEN

The Work Goes On

Administration, Management, and Leadership

The literature on leadership—and academic leadership in particular—is voluminous but in the main, unread. It continues to explore answers to such basic questions as what leadership is, how it should be taught, or even whether it *can* be taught. Perhaps the subject does not easily permit much fundamental clarification.[1] Nevertheless, helpful distinctions can be made among the three terms academic administration, academic management, and academic leadership.

In brief, academic administration is "running the shop by the book," academic management requires taking deliberate steps to change how the book is written, and academic leadership involves promulgating the values and visions that give the overall effort its meaning and direction.

Our thanks go to Dr. Kent G. Alm, former Commissioner of Higher Education for the State of North Dakota for clarifying these distinctions. Let's look quickly at each concept.

Every institution has a considerable number of policies and procedures. Most of them are written, although some may be matters more of tradition—"it's always been done this way"—than of record in committee minutes or elaboration in a faculty handbook or collective bargaining agreement. Through determining and faithfully executing these policies and procedures, the dean and provost, in "running the shop by the book," will be contributing significantly to preventing uncertainty and to maintaining the confidence and trust of faculty and students. Such reliable academic administration is a matter of no small importance.

However, the "book"—that is, the policies and procedures already in place—should never be considered good enough. One individual or another can be counted on to present an exception to established custom. Likewise, circumstances are always changing, in small if not in large ways. Consequently, there are always matters that need revision, clarification, and redirection. Academic management consists of designing and of taking the steps to bring this about. The case studies presented in earlier chapters illustrate the variety of challenges in managing the academic enterprise.

The case studies and responses make it clear that there are no pat answers to many of the problems and dilemmas faced by deans and provosts. Problems, at least, have solutions. Dilemmas, on the other hand, must often be lived with until the variables change or a long-range plan can take effect. The case studies and responses also show that considerable divergence in attitudes, strategies, and tactics must be available as the dean or provost seeks to solve a problem or live with a dilemma. A periodic re-reading of case studies and responses can refurbish the academic officer's conceptual tool box and bring forward thoughts and associations that might otherwise lay dormant even as the officer struggles to make them visible.

The case studies and responses, when taken together, demonstrate that the chief academic officer—college dean in a small institution, university provost in a large one—is a person who worries about and interfaces with the entire academic community. No problem or dilemma is off-limits if it involves the well being of the institution. Because this is true, consideration of case studies of the types presented here along with the responses to them should help broaden and deepen the point of view and attitude of the academic officer for dealing with whatever the next issue might be.

As a result of the quick turnover of frequently unrelated issues, deans and provosts often find themselves pulled in many directions at once. Even within a given issue, the dean or provost may find his or her interests and commitments being pulled in opposite directions. Although this is a natural consequence of the positions they hold, an overdose can cause stress and build anxiety, contributing to early burn out. Important coping strategies include effective delegation, widespread consultation, and judicious use of committees.

As academic management continues to evolve, use of these strategies will be helpful. Ultimately, though, it is the dean or the provost who must see that the chosen instruments are in fact working. Such management attention is indispensable for the health of the community.

Academic leadership, on the other hand, is usually not subject to codification. As a term, it is difficult to define, but is likely a product of one's personal values, visions, and practices. There are likely to be discernable differences between the genuine article and lesser species. For instance, authoritarian postures can for awhile masquerade as leadership, but in the long run will be uncovered as lacking authenticity. Similarly, encouraging vitality by pitting one group against another may work in the short term and also bolster personal power. In the long term, however, it will fragment rather than strengthen the institution. On the other hand, adopting a low profile and permitting folks to follow their own paths can be just as disastrous.

As Eble and McKeachie observe, "it is difficult to describe just what constitutes effective leadership. Like effective teachers, effective leaders come in all sizes and shapes, and have different styles and different ways of getting their way and helping others get theirs."[2] Whatever one's style, however, deliberate efforts must occur to make one's values and goals visible to others and empowering of their activities.

Power does seem to be more effectively engaged if mutuality of interests is recognized. Power itself is inadequately conceptualized if it is regarded simply as the ability to exercise influence over others. For power is also, and equally, the ability to be affected by others. This second dimension reflects the fact that no individual is independent of a community that contributes to him or her, and vice versa. Accordingly, conceptions of power that stress dominance or instrumental uses within a zero-sum context are inadequate, no matter how prevalent they may be. Maximization of individual good contributes to the good of the community, which in turn strengthens many more individuals.

Sources of Help

Wise leaders make use of assistance from a variety of areas. For instance, the various documents collected in the AAUP *Redbook* should be consulted regularly, both as potential sources of help and as reminders of traditional faculty understandings of appropriate procedures and values. The AAUP statements on ethics and responsibility could be profitably consulted and cited in the case studies dealing with faculty intimacies, faculty consulting and entrepreneurship, and grievance issues. Of course, some issues— such as the role of program redirection or termination in the release of tenured faculty members—are either not presented in the *Redbook* or may be treated from only one of several possible points of view. With regard to several other concepts—such as the equating of financial exigency with imminent financial collapse of the whole institution, thereby preventing any significant chance of avoiding it—the *Redbook* seems unrealistic or fuzzy. However, the AAUP statements on the traditional safeguards of academic freedom and due process have, on balance, served the profession quite well.

Likewise, the practice of periodic evaluation of senior faculty performance can be a significant management resource, and should not be overlooked. An institutionalized system of regular peer evaluation of tenured faculty can go far toward preventing and offsetting the stagnation and sluggishness often associated with an aging faculty. At many, if not most, institutions the bulk of evaluation activity is directed at probationary faculty, a steadily decreasing percentage of the whole faculty. This "frontloading" is neither serving the developmental needs of the majority of the faculty well nor contributing to a strengthened collegiality.

Several of the case studies pointed to the need for periodic evaluation of senior faculty performance. Departmental responsibility can be strengthened, student complaints identified and avoided, conflict over the roles of research and public service re-

duced, and the introduction of merit pay facilitated through regular
and comprehensive attention by peers to individual faculty members' accomplishments and plans. Without such a system, continued faculty development is likely to be episodic and spotty.

Various financial and budgeting techniques can provide other
sources of help. The case studies on crossing disciplinary boundaries and on continuing education illustrated the importance of
accounting mechanisms in the reward structure. Sharing of indirect cost recoveries can be an excellent motivational strategy by
recognizing and encouraging those engaged in sponsored research
activities. Formulas differ, but a common practice is for the dean
or provost to return a generous percentage of funds recovered to
those departments originating the proposals, while maintaining
centrally a sum as seed money for new projects elsewhere within
the institution.

Faculty committees can be another source of help, if things
break right. Clearly, the dean or provost cannot work for long
without them. On most issues, committees can be a significant
source of insight and a valuable mechanism for securing faculty
ownership of new proposals and developments. The responses to
the case study on experiential education illustrated the contributions committees can make to the implementation of change
and to the formulation of policy. The role of committees in the
changing of attitudes may be crucial. The liability of committees
is their unpredictability. Sometimes sluggish, sometimes seemingly downright perverse, committee direction is taken for granted
by the dean or provost only at his or her peril. The occasional
committee report may need to be accepted and then shelved—
or even corrected by another committee!

Sometimes the faculty themselves will expect or demand such
additional consideration of an issue. Colleges and universities have
considerably more than their share of articulate and verbally ori-
ented individuals. Often these are individuals with a keen interest
in having their say and seeing it done. Frequently, of course, the
futures they sketch are in various ways incompatible, and one
cancels out another. The complexity of individual agents in potential conflict is then augmented and compounded by departmental, divisional, and/or school and college perspectives. Too

many decision-makers make for both excitement and instability. The case studies dealing with athletics provided a clear illustration of this problem.

Additional sources of help are the higher education associations and the growing literature on administration and management. It is usually helpful for deans and provosts to become involved in the associations relating to their type of institution—for example, the Association of American Colleges (AAC) for the liberal arts colleges, the American Association of State Colleges and Universities (AASCU) for public institutions, the National Association of State Universities and Land Grant Colleges (NASULGC) for land grant institutions, the American Association of Community and Junior Colleges (AACJC) for two-year institutions, etc. Deans and provosts should also involve themselves with organizations that seek to serve the entire higher education spectrum such as the American Association For Higher Education (AAHE) and the American Council On Education (ACE). These, as well as associations of administrators and disciplinary societies, often have interesting meetings and worthwhile workshops and publish relevant journals.

One of the ironies in academe is that deans and provosts are kept too busy to read the growing literature on administration, management, and leadership. The very people who could profit most from this literature often see it last, or not at all. Deans and provosts generally acquire the habit of "keeping up with the literature" in their fields as faculty members. It is unfortunate that the quick pace of events in their positions deprives them of the time and energy to continue that practice as academic officers. For those who do, there are many instructive, rewarding, and therapeutic pages to be turned. A visit to one's campus library will turn up dozens of useful books and journals. Their periodic perusal is likely to contribute to the well-being of any dean or provost. Of course, some situations are straightforward power plays and must be faced as such. The case studies on the looming censure vote and the issues surrounding the acceptance of outsiders presented situations for which the literature is unlikely to be of immediate help. In these cases the sympathetic ear of a trusted friend may provide more help than anything in print.

Sources of Trouble

Compounding the turbulence generated by the pace of events is the increasing uncertainty inherent in the information overload of today. Although some campuses are still struggling to set up basic institutional research mechanisms, other institutions are suffering from an excess of data and an insufficiency of information. Academic officers at these campuses must pass the data through various screens and filters before it becomes intelligible and manageable to them. Yet, such screening may block out or obscure precisely those patterns one most needs to see. As the case study on technology and networking illustrated, turf disputes can complicate the process of securing information as readily as they can impede the making of decisions.

Likewise, the closer ties today between the campus and society can bring mixed benefits. On the one hand, these ties can generate increased resources for the college or university. On the other hand, they can also threaten its independence. For instance, the increasing interest of state governors and legislators in promoting regional economic diversification and development can generate strong pressures on institutions and faculty to neglect students' educational good by attending instead to fostering corporate connections and research arrangements. Conflicts of commitment and of interest can develop in institutions without traditions for handling them. Relations with regional industries and agencies can create difficulties for academic officers. The case study on faculty entrepreneurship and the one on the state coordinating office gave concrete illustrations of the conflicts these relations produce in many institutions. Similarly, the case studies on accreditation and on Puerto Rican studies provided examples of other types of pressures that external constituencies can bring to bear on an institution and hence on its academic officers.

While other, unforseen sources of trouble can be counted on to emerge, relative constants in the mix are the episodic and nonroutine incidents that the human condition generates and inflicts. Examples of such troubles at the individual level include cases of chronic ill health, of marital and family difficulty, and of various forms of substance abuse and addiction. Each of these can create poignant situations and pose dilemmas for academic officers, as the case study on the alcoholic dean made clear.

Other matters may be rooted in financial developments. Program reduction and redirection or institutional financial exigency can create their share of lawsuits, as well as individual despair. Having to respond to the unemployed former full professor applying for the assistant professor position is one example of the latter.

Of course, other incidents are rooted more in communal than individual or financial complexities. For instance, the concerned citizen with his or her appeal to community standards in protest or in condemnation of faculty and/or student art work comes readily to mind. Then, when the offending paintings, graphics, or film are indeed more than simply lewd, difficult battles over academic freedom and social probity will have to be joined.

Coalitions

Coalitions among the various constituencies of the academic officer must be cultivated in order to assemble and then to release new institutional energies as circumstances change. Relationships of mutual respect among them must be negotiated, and political skills in nurturing and facilitating must be exercised, as the respondents to the case study on continuing education observed. Attention must be paid as much to the way things get done as to what is produced. Good process, on the other hand, frequently requires that an appropriate structure be used or that a new one be developed.

In this connection, leadership style is quite important, as authoritarian or directive approaches are unlikely to be effective. A team leader approach emphasizing and yielding shared influence is far more likely to facilitate creativity and innovation. This style involves risk and uncertainty, but it presupposes that the best solutions to problems come from interactions with other administrators, faculty, and staff, as the case study on introducing merit pay suggested. Such an approach empowers others, and so offers the greater likelihood of favorable outcomes. The key is broad participation and collaboration.

Of course, coalitions are historically relative in nature and are contingent upon a variety of circumstances. Academic units and institutions as a whole are historical entities and go through different states and cycles. A key part of administrative leadership is recognizing where people are in this process and adjusting strategies accordingly. For instance, proposals for curricular review and development appropriate at an institution in stable financial and enrollment circumstances may not be at all possible for one just recovering from the initiation of collective bargaining or the impact of legislative budget recissions, however important, and perhaps even necessary, such curricular reviews may otherwise be.

There must also be an underlying community of basic goals and values. Successful leaders are those who can tap common aspirations in the process of transcending the present and projecting the future. Absent common aspirations, few coalitions can be built. The challenge can be substantial, as the case study on conflict in a department reminded us. In this sense, there can be no leadership without followers who give their acceptance and consent. At the same time, however, the academic officer must think about leadership strategy, as the process is as important as the substance. The academic officer must be able to articulate the institutional mission and be comfortable with broad involvement in its implementation.

Goal Divergence and the Future

Articulating the mission of an institution of higher learning has never been easy. In the first place, such articulations must seek to hit a moving target because institutional missions do change. They evolve, enjoy developmental spurts, reach periods of mature stability, undergo senescence and decay, and change again. Second, there is an enormous amount of ambiguity inherent in the purpose of it all. Finally, there is disagreement at various levels in the constituency structure of the institution as to what the purposes are or ought to be.

Regarding the first problem, some academics who try to deal with an institution's mission may be trying to do so with too short a time-line. In many cases, the forces that have shaped an institution have been in place for a long time. The notion that they can be lightly set aside or easily changed in direction is sheer folly. This aspect of the mission problem is complicated by the recognition that the forces at work have propelled the institution along a particular evolutionary trajectory. One can see within the institution fledgling departments as well as those in robust development, stable maturity, and unrelenting decline. To a large extent, whole institutions can be fit into these same categories when viewed over a long enough time-frame. If, as some observers hold, institutional evolution has been accelerating since at least the mid-1950s, obtaining an accurate fix on the current nature of the mission at any given institution may be increasingly difficult.

If one looks at a broad array of colleges and universities, many examples of mission shifts come into view. There are community colleges seeking to preempt types of work traditionally done by four-year institutions. There are private liberal arts colleges setting up applied programs in business, engineering, social service, and whatever else they can sell. There are former teacher's colleges that became regional state universities and were headed for comprehensive doctoral programs and a broad base of research who have found that today's funding levels won't carry them further on the path they thought they were treading. There are major research universities spawning centers, institutes, and public service programs that might better be developed in a nearby community college. Some primarily undergraduate institutions are trying to compress their commitment to teaching in order to free time and energy for research and public service. Some primarily graduate institutions are becoming concerned about the inadequacy of their undergraduate programs. So it goes.

It would appear that there is a great amount of jockeying as colleges and universities seek to increase or at least maintain their market share in an increasingly competitive arena. This generates mission shifts and adds significantly to the complexity of specifying with any kind of accuracy just what the mission of a particular college or university is at any one point along its evolutionary trajectory.

The enormous amount of mission ambiguity present in many colleges and universities can readily be seen after a few hours of reading the mission statements published in their catalogues. If a random sample of catalogues are pulled from a college's library shelves and subjected to a close reading, their mission statements are likely to be seen as filled with high-flown platitudes and lacking in definitive substance. Statements such as "contributing to the development of an educated citizenry" or "assuring the employ-ability of our graduates" have a nice rhetorical ring to them that may not be well-connected to what an institution actually does or intends to do.

Several studies performed a few years ago examined a whole set of variables to determine which correlated with the quality of the graduates produced by an institution. The chilling result was that the tightest correlations were obtained with the quality of the entering students—not the size of the library, the advanced degree status of the faculty, the modernity of the equipment or physical plant, or a host of other factors! As institutions rush to embrace the "nontraditional student" and make way for those who have been "educationally disenfranchised" to ensure an adequate enrollment base, the ambiguity inherent in their missions is likely to be substantially increased.

This ambiguity is overlaid by the likely fact that purposes, missions, and goals take on quite different meanings and fall into different levels of importance among different constituencies of the institution. Richman and Farmer refer to this important phe-nomenon as "goal divergence."[3] They reported "suggested rank orderings" that illustrate the depth of the problem. They reported, for instance, that among state multiversities the first priorities were to protect the faculty and get on with research and graduate education. Then came undergraduate education, pursuit of truth, and cultural assimilation. For accrediting agencies, they show graduate education, protection of the professors and faculty benefits of the professional schools followed by undergraduate education, research, and truth. Parents and alumni on the other hand, it is suggested, want jobs for graduates, cultural assimilation, undergraduate education, and athletics ahead of graduate education and public service. The federal government is presented as being primarily interested in research, especially applied research and graduate education. State governments seem to want jobs for graduates, cultural assimilation, and undergraduate education ahead of graduate education, athletics, research, and public service. Interestingly, protection of professors and faculty benefits appear at or near the bottom for both the federal and state governments. It is suggested that employers want applied undergraduate education and applied graduate education ahead of public service, research, and cultural assimilation.

To be sure, there is room for a lot of disagreement with the way these things are ranked among the various constituencies relevant to a particular institution at any one point in its evolution. It seems clear, however, that many "significant others" important to the future of that institution will have quite different rankings. Thus, goal divergence seems to us to be quite real, quite important, and often ignored by those seeking to articulate the mission of an institution of higher learning. It is our view that goal divergence is here to stay and that it is a powerful factor in influencing the nature of the future work of deans and provosts.

Given the likely continuation and importance of goal divergence, what can be said about the future of academic leadership? The nature of academic administration will almost certainly remain the same. By contrast, academic management seems very much to be in the process of fundamental change.

Academic administration—seeing to the execution of policies and procedures already firmly in place—will remain both unexciting and critical to daily routines. Faithful attention to detail will keep the institution running. Neglecting it is a sure recipe for inefficiency, disorganization, and eventual disaster. Trustworthy and reliable administration will remain unsung and uncelebrated except in its absence.

More changes are in store for academic management, at least

so far as provosts and chief academic officers are concerned. Those deans who are also chief academic officers—as they are at smaller institutions—will probably find themselves confronting the same conflicts on resource allocation with which they are already familiar. Then, as now, goal divergence will make large demands on management abilities. Within universities, however, more power seems destined to flow to the various schools and colleges and to the deans who direct them. It is they, not the provost, who will be controlling the revision, redirection, and clarification of existing policies that constitute managing the academic enterprise. The provost's work is likely to continue to shift toward developing adequate mechanisms for ensuring that the deans are appropriately doing the institution's work.

The technological revolution is assuring that information of all kinds is much more complete and accessible. The computer now makes possible at the college or school level the collection and analysis of data that were once available only centrally. Knowledge of such information is an important source of power and will strengthen the hand of the dean at the expense of the provost.

Increasingly unable to control, the provost will probably move more in the direction of facilitating. He or she will doubtless still play key roles in confirming budget decisions and allocations, but increased access by others to information will surely restrict the management discretion of the chief academic officer. Facilitating and enabling the work of others will likely be the key terms used to describe the expectations held by others for the provost of tomorrow. As management discretion is passed to or assumed by the deans, the provost is more likely than ever to emerge as an academic leader, a role now too often swamped by the demands of administration and management.

One thing, at least, is reasonably clear and quite certain. The kinds of work deans and provosts do is continuing to diversify. As exemplified by the case studies and responses in the preceding chapters, this work will continue to call for clear vision, firm dedication, and high levels of focusable energy. Whatever the future of the academy holds, deans and provosts, in seeking to better manage the academic enterprise, will help to facilitate its continuing development.

Notes

1. Madeleine F. Green, "Developing New Leaders: What Are We Trying To Do?" in *Leaders For A New Era: Strategies for Higher Education*, ed. Madeleine F. Green (New York: Macmillan, forthcoming).
2. Kenneth E. Eble and Wilbert J. McKeachie, *Improving Undergraduate Education Through Faculty Development* (San Francisco: Jossey-Bass, 1985), p. 211.
3. Barry M. Richman and Richard N. Farmer, *Leadership, Goals, and Power in Higher Education* (San Francisco, Jossey-Bass, 1976), pp. 214–216.

Index